A PRACTICAL
GUIDE TO
SOUL WINNING

A PRACTICAL GUIDE TO SOUL WINNING

Charles Arthur Crane

College Press Publishing Company, Joplin, Missouri

Library of Congress Catalog Card Number: 87-72712
International Standard Book Number: 0-89900-220-X

TABLE OF CONTENTS

ILLUSTRATIONS

DEDICATION

This volume is dedicated in loving memory of two members of the staff of First Christian Church in Caldwell, Idaho.

Joyce Rorabaugh served the church for over twenty-five years as secretary, the last five as my personal secretary. She loved the church and served many of those years without adequate pay. Her untimely death in 1981 left the church devoid of one of its most loyal servants. She has been greatly missed.

Tom Sprague served the church in a variety of ways: deacon, elder, and then Minister of Membership. Tom loved the church deeply. He served so well until his death in March of 1982 at the age of forty-seven.

Both Joyce and Tom suffered from cancer. At Joyce's funeral Tom's words were, "Who would have thought that Joyce would have gotten to see Jesus before me." His cancer was diagnosed before hers. They will be cherished in our memory until we are again united in glory!

Dr. Charles A. Crane

INTRODUCTION

Several years ago while trying to select a textbook to use in the seminary classroom, I was made aware of the lack of comprehensive books on the subject of soul winning. While there are many good books in the field, each has its own weaknesses. Some used manipulative methods, some espoused false doctrine, all left some important area untouched. Both Charles McNeeley, my associate, and I said, "Wouldn't it be great if we had one book that we could give to the students that really covered most of the areas that need covering." This is not to suggest that this book covers all areas, but that its scope is much wider than what is presently available.

The scope of this book is wide. It begins with the theology that undergirds the work of personal evangelism. What we do to evangelize must be rooted in a proper theology. If it is not, then ultimately it must fail. Just what is the most basic purpose of the church? Is that purpose tied up in the will of God?

An effort is made to tie in personal evangelism with some of the basic findings of the church growth experts. Too often workers have been asked to endeavor against insurmountable odds. A basic understanding of church growth principles should help to work around some of these roadblocks.

Much that has been called evangelism has not been founded in a careful Bible exegesis. One or more pertinent ingredients are left out of the teaching process. One of the commands of Jesus is neglected, or teachings are read into the gospel that really are not there. A proper Biblical basis must be found.

The last step is simple and practical methodology. If the plan is not simple, many will not be able to fit into it. The intention is to provide simple non-technical language and practice. If these goals have been reached, then I will be happy and my prayer will have been answered.

The book is a result of over 20 years experience in the area of personal evangelism. Many have been more successful or enlightened, possibly, but few can honestly claim that they have been more diligent in effort. The methods suggested have accounted for hundreds and hundreds of converts. These converts are in places of leadership across the land today. These principles have made strong growing churches even in difficult areas such as Salt Lake City, Utah.

It is hoped that the book will provide a useful tool for the Bible college and seminary professor. I do not even hope that it will meet the needs of all, or that it will have everything any one person wants, but I do hope that it will place together many of the things that are necessary to take a small, struggling or dying church and turn it into a living, loving, growing church.

The book should be useful for preachers. Many times I have wished for a book from which I could gain practical ideas for my own ministry. Instead, I have had to forge ideas in the fires of experience. This is the hard way. The Lord only knows where my ministry might have been if I had been given practical tools when I began. This is not an accusation against my teachers, but we should expect progress in education and practice. As new ideas come, they must be shared.

The book should have a decided usefulness for elders and deacons in the church. It certainly is not too technical for any person with 2-4 years of high school. It is directed towards the widest possible audience.

I hope it will also have a utility for the average person in the church pew. Maybe, if we finally motivate the average Mr. Christian to the work of the gospel, the church will get off of dead center and take the world as it did in the first century.

The book is a book on soul winning, but it is more than *just* a book on soul winning. The scope is toward a New Testament church—one rooted in careful scholarship, proper theology, exegesis, and simple practice.

Several people have been a help to me. Charles McNeely, of Lincoln Christian Seminary, Lincoln, Illinois, helped to formulate ideas and concepts as we team-taught there. Ben Merold of Eastside Christian Church, Fullerton, California, has been an encouragement to me and I have learned from his practical ways. All of my professors in college and seminary have had an important part. My wife, Margaret, and children, Carol, Douglas, and Steven, have been most patient with me while I have devoted days and nights to seeking the lost. My secretaries, Joyce Rorabaugh, Laura White, and Marilyn Martin, have been of great value in typing, correcting, punctuating, and encouraging. May God now add His blessing to the saving of souls.

1

THE PURPOSE OF THE CHURCH

"But now abide faith, hope, love, these three: but the greatest of these is love." I Corinthians 13:13

On a dangerous seacoast where shipwrecks often occur there was a crude little lifesaving station. The building was just a hut, and there was only one boat, but the few devoted members kept a constant watch over the sea, and with no thought for themselves went out day and night tirelessly searching for the lost. Many lives were saved by this wonderful little station, so that it became famous. Some of those who were saved, and various others in the surrounding area, wanted to become associated with the station and give of their time and money and effort for the support of its work. New boats were bought and new crews trained. The little lifesaving station grew.

Some of the members of the lifesaving station were unhappy that the building was so crude and poorly equipped. They felt that a more comfortable place should be provided as the first refuge of those saved from the sea. So they replaced the emergency cots with beds and put better furniture in the enlarged building. Now the lifesaving station became a popular gathering place for its members, and they decorated it beautifully and furnished it exquisitely, because they used it as a sort of club. Fewer members were now interested in going to sea on lifesaving missions, so they hired lifeboat crews to do this work. The lifesaving motif still prevailed in this club's decoration, and there was a liturgical lifeboat in the room where the club initiations were held. About this time a large ship was wrecked off the coast, and the hired crews brought in boatloads of cold, wet, and half-drowned people. They were dirty and sick, and some of them had black skin and some had yellow skin. The beautiful new club was in chaos. So the property committee immediately had a shower house built outside the club where victims of shipwreck could be cleaned up before coming inside.

At the next meeting, there was a split in the club membership. Most of the members wanted to stop the club's lifesaving activities as being unpleasant and a hindrance to the normal social life of the club. Some members insisted upon lifesaving as their primary purpose and pointed out that they were still called a lifesaving station. But they were finally voted down and told that if they wanted to save the lives of all the various kinds of people who were shipwrecked in those waters, they could begin their own lifesaving station down the coast. They did.

As the years went by, the new station experienced the same changes that had occurred in the old. It evolved into a club, and yet another lifesaving station was founded. History continued to repeat itself, and if you visit that sea coast today, you will find a number of exclusive clubs along that shore. Shipwrecks are frequent in those waters, but most of the people drown![1]

The above parable certainly points out the need for us to have in mind clearly what the purpose of the church is. Many people do not have in mind what God was about in the church. It seems necessary that we settle this issue before we go on to matters of how to go about this mission or purpose of the church.

The Bible speaks of God's purpose in the church.

Also we have obtained an inheritance, having been predestined according to His purpose who works all things after the counsel of His will, to the end that we who were the first to hope in Christ should be to the praise of His glory. In Him also we have obtained an inheritance, having been predestined according to His purpose who works all things after the counsel of His will, to the end that we who were the first to hope in Christ should be to the praise of His glory. In Him, you also, after listening to the message of truth, the gospel of your salvation—having also believed, you were sealed in Him with the Holy Spirit of promise, who is given as a

---

1. This parable originally appeared in an article by Theodore O. Wedel, "Evangelism — the Mission of the Church to Those Outside Her Life," *The Ecumenical Review*, October, 1953, p. 24. The above is a paraphrase of the original.

pledge of our inheritance, with a view to the redemption of God's own possession, to the praise of His glory.[2]

God does have a purpose: to redeem His own possession in order to bring Him praise and honor. God's purpose in the church is to restore man to harmony and fellowship with Him. Three things must be changed if this harmony is to be restored in the church, and the church is to realize its purpose of reaching men for Jesus Christ. But let's not get ahead of our story. Let's start at the beginning.

If a guest came to the average church and later was asked, "What is the purpose of the church?" What would he say? He might say, "It is an effort to get a perfect count on Bibles," or he might say, "It's an effort to see how many people they can get to come," or he might respond, "The church is trying to raise money for their new building." If the same person attended a Board meeting, what would be his impression? He might come away with the thought that it was discussion of profit and loss, or that the purpose of the church was to buy a new typewriter or raise money for some project within the church. Would he understand what the purpose of the church really was from observing this function in the life of the local church?

The purpose of the church is found in the purpose of God mentioned in the book of Ephesians. This purpose is seen clear back in the beginning of creation in the Garden of Eden. God created man in the beginning for fellowship. God wanted this fellowship with His creatures. He made them creatures of beauty with whom He could commune, creatures made in His own image so that they could love, being worthy of His companionship. So He made man in His own likeness; fellowship was good until rebellion and sin came in. Instead of this fellowship being realized, as God had planned to the blessedness of both God and man, because sin came fellowship was broken with God. So God brought into being a plan to bring man back into association with Him. Prophet, priest, and king were for the purpose of restoring fellowship with God. At one time it was necessary for God to destroy all

---

2. Ephesians 1:11-14, New American Standard Bible.
All scripture references will be from the New American Standard Bible, (La Habra, California: The Lockman Foundation 1960, 1962, 1963, 1968, 1971, 1972, 1973, 1975, 1977.)

but eight souls and start all over again. Finally, in His plan, He sent His only Son to save the lost and bring them back to fellowship again with Him. Everything that Jesus did was for this purpose of restoring fellowship. In the gospel of John, God is actually declaring His purpose in Jesus Christ.

> Let not your heart be troubled; believe in God, believe also in Me. In My Father's house are many dwelling places; if it were not so, I would have told you; for I go to prepare a place for you. And if I go and prepare a place for you, I will come again, and receive you to myself; that where I am, there you may be also.[3]

God is pointing out that His purpose is to bring many back into union with Him. Ephesians 1:11 calls it His purpose. In verse 14, it is called the redemption of His own possession. So the purpose of God is seen in the purpose of the church to restore man to fellowship with God; to take him from the sea of life where he is wrecked and ruined back into the safety of His church, back into His kingdom, and ultimately into heaven.

We understand then, that God will not do the changing or must not do the changing if fellowship is to be restored, but man must change if he is to have association with God. "Light cannot have fellowship with darkness."[4] The church's purpose is to get sinful man so that he can walk with the sinless Christ. In order for this to take place certain changes must be made. What are these changes? Nicodemus posed the question long ago: "How can a man be born when he is old?"[5] The question is a very important one. Nicodemus probably understood more clearly what Jesus was talking about and did not suppose He was speaking only of a physical birth. Nicodemus was asking in essence, "How can I, when I have messed up my life in sin, get back into fellowship with the sinless God?" In order for this to take place, three changes must be made for man to have fellowship with God.

How could I get a piece of cork to sink of its own will? Cork by nature, floats. In order for it to sink of its own will, its properties must be changed. It must be made more dense than water and when this is ac-

---

3. John 14:1-3.
4. II Corinthians 6:14.
5. John 3:4.

complished, then cork will sink. So man must be changed. His properties, his nature, must be changed. There are three things that the church must work to change in the lives of people in order to realize God's purpose for mankind.

The first is the object of man's faith. All people have faith. Can you imagine a person driving down the road and stopping at each bridge to check with tape measure and slide rule to see if the bridge would hold his compact car? Certainly not. We trust the engineers who build the bridges and almost always find that our faith is well founded. We have faith in our car brakes as we rush up to a stop sign and screech to a halt. We have faith in our banks, our druggist, our money, our phones.

The thing that makes men different is the object of their faith. If a man's faith is in his money, he will be a stingy penny-pincher. If he trusts God he will not worry about trivial matters of food, clothing, and drink. When we really have faith in God, it makes a vast difference in our action; we trust, we obey, we live quite differently. We are not worried about depression or recession because of our faith. The difference between the faithful Christian and the unfaithful person is faith.

We ask the questions, "How does a person go about getting faith?" "How can the church impart faith?" Romans is clear when it says, "So faith comes from hearing, and hearing by the word of Christ."[6] It sounds almost too simple, yet is is true; a study of the scriptures brings faith and change in the lives of people.

The church, in order to be about the purpose of God, must be a faith-producing organization. The writer of Hebrews says the Bible is "living and active."[7] Certainly it is. The living word is powerful. Sunday School, prayer meetings, and church attendance are faith builders. Bible study is a part of faith building. A church must then be, first and foremost, committed to a proclamation of the word of God, if it is to be a faith-building church with a goal of restoring fellowship with God. "Without faith, it is impossible to please God.[8]

The second object of a person's life that must change is that of his love. Remember the first commandment given in Matthew, "You shall love the Lord, your God, with all your heart and all your soul and with

---

6. Romans 10:17.
7. Hebrews 4:12.
8. Hebrews 11:6.

all your might."[9] That is a fine, noble ideal.

It might be well to observe that men, all men, love. The difference is what they love. Some love money, horses, themselves. Don't make any mistake about it, all men love something. Love gives direction. When a boy begins to love, it changes the direction of his whole life. He will begin washing behind his ears, brushing his teeth, combing his hair, without being told. In order then for us to bring the wonderful fellowship that we should have with God, there must be a Godly love. Jesus said, "If you love me, you will keep my commandments."[10]

You ask, "How does this love come?" God is the source of love. "God is love,"[11] Jesus said. "And I, if I be lifted up from the earth, will draw all men to myself."[12] Love comes as a gift from God.

Love grows. When a person first becomes a Christian, he most likely will not love as much as one who has been a Christian for many years. Love in marriage must grow. When a man first meets the person who later becomes his wife, he thinks that he loves her deeply and probably does, but after the couple has gone through several years of life, had several children, gone through trials and sacrifice together, their love grows.

In conversion, one thinks he loves God a lot, but when he has lived for the Lord, grown in Christ, sacrificed and suffered for Him, his love grows. The new Christian hardly understands what love is all about in comparison to the seasoned saint with many years service to Christ. The price that a person pays or is willing to pay is an indication of his love. God loved us so much that He was willing to give His most priceless gift, His son, Jesus Christ. What love costs is a measure of that love. The reason people love their children is that children cost a great deal, not only in money, but in personal sacrifice and suffering. If we got babies without cost or sacrifice they would be almost meaningless to us, but because they cost us dearly, we value them a lot. Our love will grow in relationship to our sacrifice for Jesus Christ.

During the race riots in Detroit there was a picture on the front page of a newspaper showing an old gray-haired man and woman standing

---

9. Matthew 22:37.
10. Luke 14:23.
11. I John 4:8.
12. John 12:32.

looking at the burned out ruins of their grocery store. The caption under the picture said, "If you had put as much into that corner as we had, you would not have burned it down." So with the church. Those who have put a lot into her will not want to tear her down. What our faith costs has a lot to do with how much we value it.

The boy whose father buys him a new car, certainly will not treasure or care for that car as well as the boy who works hour after hour to provide and purchase his own car. Jacob worked seven years for Rachel and got Leah, and had to work seven more years for Rachel. That is evidence of real love. It cost him, but he loved her, so he was willing to work 14 years for her. You can be sure that he treasured her.

Love shows. Some love money more than they love the church. They are stingy and will work on Sunday without cause. You can tell the people who love the lodge more than the church. They will skip the board meeting or church meeting for lodge meetings. You can tell when people love fishing or golf more than God by what they put first. When they love the Lord most, they will be at the Lord's Table on Sunday.

Love grows by sacrifice. As a Christian sacrifices for the Lord, and invests time and effort in the building of the local church, its calling program, its teaching program, and the various aspects of outreach and mission work, that person will grow to love Christ and the church.

The third and last thing that God is doing for mankind through the church is restoring or building proper hope into people's lives. Our nation has had its hope in the United Nations, big bombs, planes, treaties, strategy, and money. This is one reason why we are in such a mess today. We write on our money, "In God We Trust," but too often in our hearts we trust ourselves. Paul's hope was in the resurrection, "But now Christ has been raised from the dead, the first fruits of those who are asleep." [13] Now if a person does not have faith and love, he cannot have hope; he is really hopeless.

The author was visiting with an elderly saint of God. She was in her ninetieth year, infirm and in declining health, but was as cheerful as anyone could be. Why? It was a matter of hope. She had been a Christian for seventy-eight years and a hard worker in the kingdom and she had the same hope that the song writer had who wrote, "My hope is

---

13. I Corinthians 15:20.

built on nothing less than Jesus' blood and righteousness."[14] What a wonderful and sure hope.

The suicidal person has often lost hope, but the Christian has lasting hope because of his trust in Jesus Christ. It is the church's responsibility to help people to have proper hope. Our hope is in the resurrection in heaven.

> In My Father's house are many dwelling places; if it were not so, I would have told you; for I go to prepare a place for you. And if I go and prepare a place for you, I will come again, and receive you to Myself; that where I am, there you may be also.[15]

That is real hope.

As a young man, the author lived in Portland, Oregon, and was courting a young lady from Coos Bay, Oregon. It was 175 miles to her house and in those days most people drove fifty-five miles per hour as a matter of necessity, because their cars could not stand much more. The closer the author got to Coos Bay, the slower the car seemed to go. Anticipation was so great that it was impossible to be sleepy. It was a matter of hope. So with the Christian's hope. As we draw nearer in faith and love to that perfect city in which dwelleth righteousness, hope takes over — the hope of seeing Jesus, the hope of seeing our loved ones, and our parents who have gone on before us. Faith and love are made perfect through hope. Worries are past and we look for the beautiful city.

So the church's responsibility is to be like a lifesaving crew, rescuing people from the sea of life, bringing them into the kingdom where they can be brought into fellowship with God. Three things are necessary in order for a person to have fellowship with God. These three things, according to the writer of I Corinthians are, "But now abide, faith, hope, and love, these three, but the greatest of these is love."[16] That is the purpose of the church. Keep this foremost in your mind, that the church's purpose is to bring people into fellowship with God. Such a noble purpose will motivate us to diligent efforts on behalf of our Lord, Jesus Christ.

---

14. Edward Mote, "The Solid Rock."
15. John 14:2-3.
16. I Corinthians 13:13.

Chapter 1 Examination

1. What is God's purpose in the church?

2. What three things need to be restored in man if God and man are to have fellowship?

3. How can a person get faith?

4. How can a person grow in love?

5. What is the basis of our hope?

6. How can faith be measured?

7. How can love be measured?

8. What is the church's responsibility in today's world?

9. In a few words, explain how the church has been diverted from its original purpose.

10. The ultimate result of the church's work will be realized in what benefit of mankind?

Note: Some of the thoughts in this chapter were prompted by a lecture in seminary given by Dr. Earl Hargrove.

2

THE NEW TESTAMENT THEOLOGY OF CHURCH GROWTH

"What man among you, if he has a hundred sheep and has lost one of them, does not leave the ninety-nine in the open pasture, and go after the one which is lost, until he finds it?" Luke 15:4

God wants His church to grow. Underlying the whole message of God's purpose is the fact that God expects His church to be about an equipping ministry, equipping people for service. This service is bringing people into the kingdom. The Ephesians writer said:

And He gave some as apostles, and some as prophets, and some as pastors and teachers, for the equipping of the saints for the work of service, to the building up of the body of Christ.[1]

Somehow in the church, lots of teaching and equipping has been done, but little ministry or service has been accomplished. What is the problem? Possibly the problem could be illustrated by telling a story.

Once in a pizza parlor, it was observed that during a smorgasbord luncheon where one could eat all they wanted for $1.39, a man ate twenty-one pieces of chicken, a family-size pizza, four or five large

---

1. Ephesians 4:11-12.

drinks, and a great quantity of salad. He was referred to by the owner as "Little Jake." His stomach would hang down over his belt and the seat that he sat upon. He would take a chicken leg, put it in his mouth, twist it a time or two and the bone was bare. He would eat a little while, then sit back and pant, and then eat some more. He must have weighed nearly five hundred pounds.

Isn't this the sort of problem that we face in the church? We have been fed and fed with spiritual chicken, pizza, and salad, and are so glutted with food and so fat and lazy, that we do little that relates to what God's main purpose is for His church. God wants His church to grow. It is the thing closest to His heart. In the New Testament Church we have the finest and clearest doctrine anywhere. It makes sense. It appeals to the thinking person. It isn't as if the Christian did not have good sensible facts to rest his faith upon; he certainly does. Why, then, haven't we taken the world with it? Could it be that we do not have our priorities clearly in mind? What is God's number one concern? What should be our number one concern? How can we please God best? What traits will make us most like Christ, most Christian? The truth of the matter is, God does want His church to grow.

It is like the song writer said:

> Seeking the lost, yes, kindly entreating
> Wanderers on the mountain astray;
> "Come unto Me," His message repeating,
> Words of the Master speaking today.
>
> Seeking the lost, and pointing to Jesus,
> Souls that are weak and hearts that are sore;
> Leading them forth in ways of salvation,
> Showing the path to life evermore.
>
> Thus I would go on missions of mercy,
> Following Christ from day unto day;
> Cheering the faint, and raising the fallen;
> Pointing the lost to Jesus, the Way.[2]

That is what God wants His Church doing. That is the church's business. It should be shown in our lives, our love, and our concern.

---

2. W.A. Ogden, "Seeking the Lost."

Our commission should be seeking those who are lost.

Throughout the Bible the theme is the same. God wants the lost saved, brought into His kingdom, into the church. It is the church's responsibility. For example, Luke repeats the parable of the lost sheep which stresses God wants His church to grow.[3] While the parable's depth has not been fully explored, its truth is crystal clear. God wants the lost saved and brought into His fold. Notice that the parable says:

> What man among you, if he has a hundred sheep and has lost one of them, does not leave the ninety-nine in the open pasture, and go after the one which is lost, until he finds it.[4]

This is foreign to the life of many churches. Churches shepherd the saved, visit the saved, and see the sickly saved. The program of the average minister is so filled with the care of the ninety-nine saved that he has little time for the lost in the community. How can the church grow under these conditions? The good shepherd went looking for the one lost sheep, leaving the ninety-nine saved behind. Dare we follow Jesus' example, leaving the ninety-nine and go seeking the lost person in our community?

Notice that he left the ninety-nine in the open field or wilderness. The songwriter was wrong when she said: "There were ninety and nine that *safely lay in the shelter of the fold.* But one was out on the hills away, Far off from the gates of gold."[5] The shepherd left the sheep, according to the text, in the open pasture. Christians are still in the wilderness of sin; Christians are in the wilderness of the world. Jesus is teaching that we should leave the saved and go seek the lost. Why? He wants His church to grow. He is not willing that any should perish, but that all should come to repentance.

The songwriter really does not portray the meaning or teaching of Jesus in the song, "Hold the Fort." Why? Because the Christian is to press the battle, not sit in the fort, yet Christians have adopted this attitude of fort-holding. We must learn from Jesus to go seeking that lost person on our block, our neighbor, the lost children in our family, and

---

3. Luke 15:3-7.
4. Luke 15:4.
5. Elizabeth C. Clephane, "The Ninety and Nine."

our lost friends. We were lost, condemned, and undone. Jesus came seeking us. We were out on the sea of life but Jesus found and saved us. Our commission from Jesus Christ is that we go seek the one lost person. Certainly in our day there is not a problem of just one lost person, but multitudes of lost people.

The parable also shows the persistence that Jesus Christ wants the Christian to have. He is to seek the lost person "until he finds it." One of the very first lessons the person must learn who wants to seek the lost is persistence, "until he finds it." We say, "It is hard; I can't do it." We must learn the lesson, "until he finds it." We must zero in on the one that we would find and seek the person until we find them.

How will we feel when we know that our loved ones, our children, our friends, are lost and we could have done something about it, but we did not? How will we feel when we realize that we have done nothing, or did very little to bring people to know Jesus Christ? The song writer said:

> How can I meet Him without my loved ones;
>   How can I smile and know they are lost;
> When I see Jesus up in the glory
>   Without the souls He bought at such a cost?
>
> Time now for warning, time now for pleading,
>   Time now to weep, to cling to the cross.
> Too late in Heaven to win our loved ones;
>   Too late to pray, to weep o'er the lost.
>
> Solemn accounting, facing our Saviour.
>   Rewards receiving — suffering loss!
> Judgment set, facing Jesus in Heaven;
>   Wood, hay and stubble, burning as dross.
>
> How poor investment, in land or business;
>   What cheap returns, we'll have for our pains!
> But how wise will shine in their glory,
>   When souls appear, what eternal gain!
>
> How glad the greeting, praises and singing
>   When we meet Jesus, with all our own!
> Then will our labor seem but a trifle,
>   And all our tears and toiling be done!

Oh, bring your loved ones, bring them to Jesus!
Bring ev'ry brother and sister to Him!
When come the reapers home with the harvest,
May all our dear ones be safe gathered in![6]

The message of the parable is that the good shepherd goes looking, expending sweat and tears until he finds that one. The Master's example to the soul-winner, to the church worker, is "until he finds it." Why did Jesus leave glory? Why did He come to earth? Why was He born in a stable? Why flee to Egypt? Why did He sleep on hillsides? Why was He hated and abused? "It is a trustworthy statement, deserving full acceptance that Christ Jesus came into the world to save sinners among whom I am foremost of all."[7] That's why He went through five trials, whippings, the purple robe, the crown of thorns, the Judas' kiss, until He prayed, "Let this cup pass from me." That's why He had the pierced hands and feet, the side with spear plunged in. Why? Until He found us. As Peter says, "... not wishing for any to perish, but for all to come to repentance."[8]

When a person is brought to salvation, then there is rejoicing in heaven. "I tell you that in the same way there will be more joy in heaven over one sinner who repents than over ninety-nine righteous persons who need no repentance."[9] When a lost child is brought to Christ, there is great joy in heaven. When a lost mother or father is brought to salvation, there is great, unspeakable joy. The fatted calf of heaven is brought out, and trumpets and the bands of heaven strike up with singing because the lost is found. It is the completion of God's whole divine plan to bring man back into fellowship and harmony with Him. God's number one concern, the thing most important to God is realized. Soul-winning rejoices God.

A careful look through the Scriptures shows many examples indicating that God wants His church to grow. Jesus, by the sea of Galilee, spoke of making His disciples "fishers of men." It illustrates

---

6. John R. Rice, "Oh, Bring Your Loved Ones,": in *742 Heart-Warming Poems* (Murfreesboro, Tennessee: Sword of the Lord Publishers, 1972), stanzas 1-6, number 687.

7. I Timothy 1:15.

8. II Peter 3:9.

9. Luke 15:7.

that God wanted the apostles to be soul-winners. The lady with the lost coin, in Luke 15, who hunts and sweeps until she finds it, is an illustration of seeking that which is lost, God's concern for lost people. It is a story of soul-winning and church growth. The parable of the lost boy, in Luke 15, is really a picture of lost humanity, mired in the pigpen of sin, eating the husks of the devil's fare. It is the story of God's concern as He sits at the windows of heaven, waiting for the return of the lost boy, His lost humanity. The parable of the wedding feast bears the message to, "Go into the highways and byways and compel them to come in."[10] God's concern is that people come into His kingdom, the church.

Centuries of careful planning were involved, "But when the fullness of the time came, God sent forth His Son, born of a woman, born under the Law, in order that He might redeem those who were under the Law, that we might receive the adoption as sons."[11] "It is a trustworthy statement, deserving full acceptance, that Christ Jesus came into the world to save sinners, among whom I am foremost of all."[12] That is why Christ came, just at the right time; all the plans were ready, ready for drawing people into the kingdom of Christ. Jesus came seeking the lost. The Great Commission's message is to go to all nations, make disciples of these people, and teach these people, and baptize these people.[13] It is God's purpose that the whole world hear about Jesus Christ. The message was proclaimed publicly during the days of the early church, and from house to house. God's plan was and is to bring the message to the people's homes, a personal teaching session for everyone by personal workers, by tracts, by television, and by radio, that all may hear again and again that God is not willing that any should perish.

Zaccheus is a story of soul-winning up a tree. Matthew is the story of a tax collector won to Jesus Christ. The parables of the pearl of great price, the fish net, and on and on, are messages of God's concern for the lost.

How many people would have been won to Christ if someone had shown as much concern for them and their souls as they did for a pet or hobby? Yes, people will be in hell that could have been saved if some-

---

10. Luke 14: 23.
11. Galatians 4:4-5.
12. I Timothy 1:15.
13. Matthew 28:19-20.

one would have given them as much love as they did their dog, cat, or horse. A little white poodle resides at the author's home. She gets lots of attention from the boys and from the other members of the family. Every need of hers is lovingly supplied. Isn't it strange that many people in the world have not had as much concern shown for their eternal salvation as this little white poodle has had for her physical needs? How many eternal souls would have been saved if we would give them some love and concern, to love them into the kingdom? How many children would have been won? How many brothers and sisters could have been won? Certainly we need to pray, "Lord, forgive the Christian for his lack of concern for the lost."

The story was first told, and then a song was written, all originating in a true story. The young man of fourteen to sixteen years of age went astray in his hometown, shunning the advice of his loving parents, hurting them and ruining their home. Every sin in the book was committed by this young fellow. Finally in shame and sin he ran away from home. Several years passed when finally he came to his senses, and realized the failure of his way. He wrote home and asked his mother and father if he would be welcome if he came back home. He said in his letter that he would be coming on the evening train that ran past their back yard, where he had played as a youth. If he was welcome, they were to tie a ribbon on the oak tree that stood behind the house under which he had often played as a boy. If not welcome, no ribbon was to be tied in the tree. As the train approached, he could not bear to look for fear there would be no ribbon. He confided in an older man who sat next to him and finally asked him to look back as the train had already passed the yard. The man said, "Son, there is a ribbon tied from every branch."

God wants us to tie a ribbon to every branch of the tree of salvation to let the world know that He wants them to be saved. God wants His church to grow. The New Testament Church did grow phenomenally. This is a matter of record. Jesus spent most of His ministry with twelve men. These men were the core of His plan for growth in the church. Just before the day of Pentecost, the number of intimate disciples appears to have been about 120.[14] After the preaching of the first gospel sermon, in which salvation was preached through the blood of Jesus Christ, three thousand people accepted Christ and were baptized the

---

14. Acts 1:15.

same day. By the fourth chapter of Acts, the number of men came to be about five thousand. [15] This could mean that as many as fifteen to twenty thousand people had become Christians. We ask the question, "Why such phenomenal growth in the life of the church?" In the fourth chapter, the disciples were called "a multitude."[16] How many is a multitude? Certainly a lot of people, and yet it says in the fifth chapter, "And all the more believers in the Lord, multitudes of men and women, were constantly added to their number,"[17] indicating that the progress of the church was picking up momentum. In the sixth chapter, we read, "And the word of God kept on spreading; and the number of the disciples continued to increase greatly in Jerusalem, and a great many of the priests were becoming obedient to the faith."[18] So it not only spread rapidly among the people, but even the priests were giving themselves over to Jesus Christ. In the ninth chapter, two whole cities turned to Christ. [19]

Certainly we can say that this is an exceptional record of growth. God wanted His church to grow and the church was growing in an outstanding way. The question needs to be asked and carefully answered, "Why such growth? Why such growth in the life of the early church and often such meager growth today?" I believe the answer can be found in the methodology of Jesus and the apostles. What was the Biblical concept and practice of growth within the church?

It appears to have been the concept of one-to-one evangelism. As we observe the ministry of Jesus Christ, He called His apostles a few at a time, one here and one there, after He had had time with them as individuals.

Jesus, during His ministry, spent time with the lady at the well of Sychar, spent time having dinner with Zaccheus, spent time talking to Nicodemus, and spent time with the rich young ruler. The Lord of glory had time to spend with many individuals on a one-to-one basis. It has been said that the best teaching takes place where there is a log on which a student is sitting on one end and a teacher on the other. Jesus spent much time on a one-to-one basis with people that He taught.

---

15. Acts 4:4.
16. Acts 4:32, King James Version.
17. Acts 5:14.
18. Acts 6:7.
19. Acts 9:35.

What was the methodology used by the apostles and other church workers in the early church? Acts gives us a wonderful account of the progress of the church. Peter and John had time for one man at the Gate Beautiful who was lame from his birth.[20] The Ethiopian eunuch was led to Christ by Philip, the evangelist.[21] Saul was taught by Ananias in the ninth chapter.[22] The household of Cornelius was taught by the great apostle, Peter.[23] Lydia and her household were taught by Paul.[24] The Philippian jailer and his household were taught by Paul and Silas.[25] Apollos was taught by Priscilla and Aquila.[26] In this very short history of some of the acts of some of the apostles in the early church, it is remarkable how many one-to-one encounters the history records.

If we were to know the full extent of the work of the average Christian person in the early church, in evangelizing on a one-to-one basis, we would be amazed. The church grew because people understood the teaching of Jesus Christ. We were to go out and seek that one lost sheep, that one lost person in their community, that one person in our experience that did not know about Jesus Christ.

The basic methodology of Jesus and the apostles was not only public proclamation, but private. A great deal of time was spent by these very important people on a one-to-one basis, teaching about Christ. Jesus' commission, given to the church of today, is that He is ". . . not wishing for any to perish but all to come to repentance,"[27] and ". . . go therefore and make disciples of all the nations, baptizing them in the name of the Father and the Son and the Holy Spirit, teaching them to observe all that I commanded you; and lo, I am with you always, even unto the end of the age."[28]

The New Testament theology of church growth was public and private proclamation to those all around. When the church of today gets back to the methodology and theology of church growth that is found in the Scriptures, the church will begin to experience outstanding growth.

---

20. Acts 3:1-10.
21. Acts 8:26-36.
22. Acts 9:10-20.
23. Acts 10:1-48.
24. Acts 16:14-15.
25. Acts 16:26-34.
26. Acts 18:26.
27. II Peter 3:9.
28. Matthew 28:19-20.

Chapter 2 Examination

1. According to Ephesians 4:11-12, church leadership is to do what for the church members (saints)?

2. In the parable of the lost sheep, Luke 15:3-7, where were the ninety-nine sheep left by the Good Shepherd?

3. The parable says Jesus sought the lost sheep "until he finds it." What lesson should we learn from this?

4. According to this parable, what happens in heaven when a lost person is brought to Christ?

5. What is taught by Christ's parable of the lost coin and the lost boy? Luke 15.

6. The story of Zaccheus is a story about what?

7. The story of the parents tying ribbons on almost every branch of the old oak tree illustrates what truth for the church?

8. The early chapters of Acts shows remarkable growth in the church. What was the biblical concept that helped bring about this remarkable growth?

9. Jesus spending time with the woman at the well of Sychar, with Nicodemus, and with the rich young ruler illustrates what need today?

10. The progress of the early church was remarkable. What was one of its causes as illustrated by the man at the Gate Beautiful, the Ethiopian Eunuch, Saul taught by Ananias, and the household of Cornelius?

11. What two methods did Jesus and the Apostles use to evangelize?

12. The New Testament Theology of church growth was what?

3

CHURCH GROWTH PRINCIPLES AND RAPID CHURCH GROWTH

". . . you shall be my witnesses both in Jerusalem, and in all Judea and Samaria, and even to the remotest part of the earth." Acts 1:8

Dr. Robert G. Lee said:

I look at the map and think of the Cilician gates. Through them passed the army of Alexander the Great, with gaudy banners, shining shields, trenchant spears, sharp-edged swords, quivers full of arrows, bows strong — stringed and soldiers with mouths full of victorious bombast. But I see a little deformed Jew, the Apostle Paul, go through those gates with the gospel message, as he compassed the earth with the truths of redemption, going forth to twist the rusty hinges off the doors of nations, to put out the altar fires of Diana, to carry the banner of the Cross over a wider territory than the Roman eagles shadowed, to leave a trail of gospel glory across the Gentile world. His footsteps outweighed the footsteps of all the soldiers of Alexander's army. His pen outweighed and made greater conquests than all the army's swords — because he journeyed as a soul winner. Still, as in Paul's day, people need to be brought to Christ who saves, built up in Christ who empowers, sent out for Christ, that the unsaved shall by the saved be brought to Christ. Soul saving is the heart and soul of the work of the Church — yea, of all Christians. Nothing can be substituted for it.[1]

---

1. Robert G. Lee, *How to Lead a Soul to Christ*, (Grand Rapids, Michigan: Zondervan Publishing House, 1955), p. 12.

Since the gospel message is so great, so beneficial, so needful for the good of mankind, we must do all within our power and intelligence to spread it far and near. Our best efforts, or best planning, will be none too good. Therefore, church growth principles must be employed to move the church off dead center to its great calling.

Many of us have probably observed a person who, finding no success with certain methods, had redoubled efforts using the same methods. How often this has been the case in churches today, only God knows. When unsuccessful means are used, the person, rather than learning from his lack of success, continues on with the same thing that brought failure before.

Church growth experts have studied church movements across the world. This research is available to us today. Such church growth experts as Dr. Donald McGavran, Dr. Winn Arn, Dr. Tetsunao Yamamori, and Dr. E. LeRoy Lawson have written and given us the benefit of their experience. From the work and writings of these authors, twelve principles seem to come to the forefront.

1. THE PRINCIPLE OF KOINONIA AND GROWTH.[2]

Koinonia is a Greek term used in the scriptures and is often translated "fellowship". It has more meaning than just being together with other people, but includes the idea of warmth, love, and mutual concern. In the world today outside the church, persons can find good music, good lectureships, teaching, and seminars, and can even find companionship. In fact, most of the things offered by the church can be found outside the church, with the exception of one thing. That one thing is koinonia, the brotherly fellowship that is found by those who come into Jesus Christ. Thus, if it is going to be successful, the church must really be a place of koinonia; a place where there is mutual love and concern, where love is openly expressed and shown. In the early church they saluted one another with a holy kiss,[3] a token of affection and love. Every part in the life of the church must then be completely permeated by expressions of genuine love.

Directly related to koinonia is agape love. The Greeks used four

---

2. Acts 2:42, 44-45; 12:12.
3. Romans 16:16.

words for love. *Storge* was used for love within a family, such as between parents and children. *Phileo* meant a friendly love towards associates or friends. *Eros* was used to speak of romantic or sexual love. For the highest form of love they used the word, *agape.*

Agape is the kind of love God and Christ have for each other. It is the kind of love that caused Jesus to die for us. It is the kind of love that makes it possible for one to even love his enemies.

In John 15:17 & 19 we read: "This I command you, that you love one another. If the world hates you, you know that it has hated Me before it hated you. If you were of the world, the world would love its own. . . ." In these verses the first word for love is *agape.* Christians *agape* each other. The second word is *phileo.* The world feels friendly love for each other. The Christian achieves a much higher type of love. This *agape* love cannot be found in the world as it is a fruit of the Spirit. Galatians 5:22, "But the fruit of the Spirit is love, (i.e. *agape*)."

The deeper relationships in Christ cannot be found in the world. Since this is true we must be sure there is an atmosphere of genuine fellowship and real godly love in the body. When there is this atmosphere the church will grow.

2. INTENSITY OF BELIEF AND CHURCH GROWTH.[4]

Movements with firm convictions have been shown to grow, while those without do not grow. Conservative, fundamental churches that really preach the gospel are growing around the world. Church growth statistics demonstrate this conclusively. Those churches that feel, ". . . woe is me if I do not preach the gospel,"[5] are the churches that are showing fantastic growth. Sometimes zeal and enthusiasm are offensive to the more cultured, but those attributes make the difference between life and death as far as a church is concerned. When a church or movement realizes that to contain the joy of salvation within themselves is to lose a great deal of it, then they will begin to reach out to others with the gospel joyfully. The real enemies of church growth are the ideas of religious relativism, saying that all roads lead to the

---

4. Tetsunao Yamamori and E. LeRoy Lawson, *Introducing Church Growth,* (Cincinnati, Ohio: Standard Publishing, 1975), p. 116.
5. I Corinthians 9:16.

same place or same God and it doesn't make any difference what you believe, as long as you are sincere. They lead to apathy in religion and cause religious movements to stop growing. Where there are earnest, dedicated people interested in the truth of God, zealous for what they know is right, the church can grow. The Bible clearly teaches the need for strong beliefs.

> I solemnly charge you . . . preach the word; be ready in season and out of season; reprove, rebuke, exhort, with great patience and instruction. For the time will come when they will not endure sound doctrine; but wanting to have their ears tickled, they will accumulate for themselves teachers in accordance to their own desires; II Timothy 4:1-4.

What the Bible says has been reaffirmed by those who have studied church growth principles today. A church needs strong convictions if it is to grow.

3. RAPID CHURCH GROWTH IS ASSOCIATED WITH PEOPLE MOVEMENTS.[6]

Just what is a people movement? Let me illustrate. A Lincoln Continental pulled up in front of the church. The power window was rolled down and the woman said, "Would you baptize me?" The preacher said, "Well, I would like to visit with you a little bit about your faith in Christ." "Surely," was her reply. "Why don't you come into my office and we'll talk about it," he said. In the process of time this lady was baptized, her sister-in-law was baptized, her sister-in-law's children were baptized, her children were baptized. Then her husband was baptized, then his brother was baptized. Next it spread to the father-in-law and mother-in-law of the lady who had driven into the parking lot, and then to another brother and his wife and children. It was simply a people movement.

It has been demonstrated that the gospel moves best through families, from one family member to another. The gospel moves with power best through one strata of society. Rapid church growth of a permanent nature has often been along the lines of people movement.

---

6. Yamamori and Lawson, *Introducing Church Growth,* p. 116.

In the gospels the people movement principle is illustrated by the calling of the disciples. The message traveled from Andrew to Peter, and from Philip to Nathanael. John 1:40-45.

At Pentecost, as recorded in the second chapter of Acts, many families came to Christ. If we knew the facts, we would probably learn that these people went back to their respective countries and lands and won their families to Christ. Thus, not only the church in Jerusalem grew to fifteen to twenty thousand in a few weeks, but the gospel spread across the world. Philip preached to the Ethiopian eunuch; he became a Christian and tradition says he began a people movement that became the Coptic church that thrived until the Mohammedan Invasion in about 600 A.D.[7] The excuse that is often given of not being able to talk to our families about Jesus is a lame one, not founded in fact. It is an excuse showing that we may not yet have the mind of Christ.

The technical term for this pattern of church growth is multi-individual; individual, independent movements to Christ. It is not mass conversion or group conversion, but it is a chain reaction of conversions. It is the logical way for a church to grow. Through a stratum of society, one family member leads another family member to Christ. They in turn give support to each other as they seek to reach other members of their own family. People who come to Christ need the support of their family members within the framework of society in which they live and they find it as a people movement spreads.

What we need to learn is that people came to Christ along family lines most easily and naturally. When a child is won, then the parents, the brothers, the sisters, and so on through the society structures in which the people live, the gospel is spreading as a people movement.

4. SOCIAL STRUCTURES RECEPTIVITY AND CHURCH GROWTH.[8]

Churches have lesser or greater successes in certain strata of society,

---

7. Acts 8:27.

8. Yamamori and Lawson, *Introducing Church Growth*, p. 118. (Acts 6:5 The men have Greek names indicating they had a large Greek population in the church Wherever the church went the gospel was first preached to the Jews. Receptivity was a prime consideration in evangelism.)

for example, upper class, lower class, or middle class individuals. Some may draw almost all white, others almost all black. The church needs to determine where it has been most effective and put its major emphasis there. Growing churches need to know their communities; they must take every means to find the open doors. When they have found them, then they should work in the pockets of receptivity, reaching out for Jesus Christ. Most churches will find that there are certain ethnic groups with whom they will have little influence. It does not mean that they are not concerned with those people, but that they should expend their efforts where social structures will permit them to be most received. There will be areas of receptivity whether it be along economic lines or ethnic lines, and they should seek to find these areas and concentrate their work in these areas.

5. POST-BAPTISMAL TEACHING AND CHURCH GROWTH.[9]

This has to do with closing the back door of the church as well as training the ones converted to Christ. Jesus said that we were to go and preach the gospel to every creature, baptizing them in the name of the Father, the Son and the Holy Spirit, and then teaching them to observe all things that He had commanded. One doesn't need to become perfect to be baptized. It is a birth, a beginning, entering into a living relationship with Jesus Christ, but as a baptized believer, one must grow.[10] It is necessary for the man in the pew to learn and he must become involved in the mission of the church. If the church is going to grow, it must be by the converts.

The Bible teaching is clearly stated. Matthew 28:20 says, "teaching them." The new converts are to be carefully instructed. Timothy was told, "In pointing out these things to the brethren, you will be a good servant of Christ Jesus . . . prescribe and teach these things." I Timothy 4:6 & 11. "All scripture is inspired by God and is profitable for teaching, for reproof, for correction, for training in righteousness; that the man of God may be adequate, equipped for every good work." II Timothy 3:16-17.

---

9. Yamamori and Lawson, *Introducing Church Growth*, p. 120.
10. Ephesians 4:15; I Peter 2:2; II Peter 3:17-18.

The New Testament is literally full of admonitions to study and teach. Every member of the body can be equipped for ministry and evangelism. The new convert grows in faith by being taught the word. Romans 10:17.

Without a doubt, we have taught by action and inference that only the super-educated can do the work of evangelism. Nothing is wrong with education, but it is not necessary to study years and years before one can become a really effective soul winner and church worker.[11] When a person is baptized, he should be inducted into the teaching ministry of the church and be trained and mobilized to win those around him for Christ. Post-baptismal teaching is imperative to church growth.

6. CHURCH POLICY AND CHURCH GROWTH.[12]

It has been demonstrated that if a church is to grow it must have a policy directed towards and constantly emphasizing the need for growth. If we were to be evaluated by an independent church evaluating team, what would they say about our church goals? What are these goals? Would it be feeding the hungry? Feeding the hungry is important. Would it be clothing the naked? That, too, is important. But what is our chief task? The great commission speaks clearly of what our task is to be, Matthew 28:19-20. The early Christians understood what was expected. "Therefore, those who had been scattered went about preaching the word." Acts 8:4. Timothy was charged to: "preach the word;" II Timothy 4:2-4. What is the chief task of the church?

Certainly the chief task is not feeding the hungry or clothing the naked; that is an outreach and a part of our Christian mission, to be sure. But the central task is to bring men and women back into fellowship with God. When we let anything else take precedence over that, we lose sight of the real goal and purpose of the church. Churches have been demonstrated to grow best when they have a clear picture of their goal, church growth, reaching the whole community, and the whole world for Christ.

---

11. Philip and Stephen, deacons, were effective teachers and preachers. Acts chapters 6, 7, & 8.

12. Yamamori and Lawson, *Introducing Church Growth*, p. 120.

41

7. THE PSYCHOLOGY OF EXPECTANCY AND CHURCH GROWTH.[13]

A lot depends upon our attitudes. If we think we cannot do something, we are defeated before we start. Optimism is a must if the church is going to grow. One of the keys to the Apostle Paul's success was his positive attitude. His words, "I can do all things through Him who strengthens me," Philippians 4:13, are characteristic of his attitudes of expectancy. The church must expect growth. The church must build enthusiasm, talk up the work, build and see the positive side of what is happening. Something positive can be said even when the situation is less than ideal. In fact, it has been pointed out that you can say something good about anybody; for example, even Satan is a hard worker. So see the bright side, and whenever things begin to move, increase your evangelistic efforts. When the efforts begin to pay off in souls saved, redouble your efforts. There is a definite relationship between expectancy and church growth.

8. THE HOLY SPIRIT AND CHURCH GROWTH.[14]

A whole book needs to be written on the Holy Spirit's part in church growth. In brief survey, to prompt individual thinking, let me suggest that the church began by the unleashing of the Holy Spirit's power at Pentecost.[15] Since that time it has been the unleashing power behind every true conversion and missionary effort in the world. The Holy Spirit is very much present in all conversions. As we look at the work that Christ has called us to do, we certainly cannot do it in our own power, but we can, through the Holy Spirit, accomplish great things. The agent behind, throughout, and in the center of conversion is the Holy Spirit. When Spirit-filled Christians begin to proclaim Jesus Christ, there will be souls saved;[16] there will be new Philips, Stephens, Pauls, and Barnabases who go out proclaiming Jesus Christ. Claim His power.

---

13. Ibid. p. 121.
14. Ibid.
15. Acts 1:8; 2:4 The apostles spoke because of the Holy Spirit's filling.
16. John 16:8-11.

Go not in your own strength, but in the strength of the Holy Spirit of God.

9. THE DYNAMIC OF INDIVIDUAL WITNESS.[17]

Great church growth is associated with a movement of individual testimony and witness. The Chief of Atua became a Christian after hearing John William's sermon. His testimony won his own and two other islands in rapid succession. Thus began the mighty tide that swept the Pacific from island to island in a few years: fifteen thousand in Tahiti; eleven thousand in the Hervey Islands; thirty-three thousand in Samoa; one hundred thousand Polynesians in thirty years; seventy thousand in New Zealand; thirty thousand in Tonga in three years; one hundred thousand in Fiji; one hundred thousand in New Ireland; and on and on. The Spirit of God was in it, but it began by a chief being won and using his personal witness immediately. Any church that wants to be really evangelistic must depend upon its members for witness, especially its new members. Any person who is a Christian should have a personal witness. Tell what happened to you. If it didn't happen, come and be converted. This witness can be used wherever you go. The church grew in the first century because of not only public but private proclamation. Paul's example was, "how I did not shrink from declaring to you anything that was profitable, and teaching you publicly and from house to house," Acts 20:20. This method can today be employed on church member and non-church member alike.

It is estimated that in the United States alone, there are one hundred million Americans who are Christians in name only, that have not really let Christ take over their lives. So, we need to talk to these people as well as those who have never even made a beginning commitment to Christ. Movements around the world are growing out of one or two people's dedicated personal witness. One woman in Formosa has been reported as having started a movement that has now grown to over fifty thousand strong.

---

17. Yamamori and Lawson, *Intro. Church Growth*, p. 121.

10. REVIVAL AND CHURCH GROWTH.[18]

Unless we have been revived, we won't have much church growth.[19] When we are really revived, directing our testimony towards friends and neighbors, we will see growth. Dr. J. Edwin Orr, while lecturing to a group of seminarians, was asked why any Christian should ever need revival. Dr. Orr, with his years of experience and his beautiful, gentlemanly way, pointed out to the group of seminarians that he had had a bath that very morning, but after being out in the humid, dusty, Illinois farm country, he was beginning to feel that he would need a bath again and he presumed that as a human he would need a bath fairly regularly for the rest of his life. So it is, he said, with revival. Revival is a matter of being revived and re-enthused with the things of the gospel of Jesus Christ. He went on to point out to the group that revival means revitalization of existing Christians. Revival means incessant Bible study, prayer, and the presence of the Holy Spirit in life. When a few Christians have been revitalized, revival will spread like wildfire; therefore, revival must be a part of church growth.

11. THE INDIGENOUS PRINCIPLE OF CHURCH GROWTH.[20]

The word "indigenous" has to do with something that belongs to a particular area or environment.[21] For example, one could speak of bananas as being indigenous to a semi-tropical or warm tropical climate. We speak of the Douglas Fir tree as being indigenous to the Cascade Mountains of Oregon and Washington. These plants belong there. This is the environment where they have been reared and where they do well. The term "indigenous," as applied to the church, means the church must satisfy the needs of the people who live in that area. The church must belong to the people who make up its membership. What others outside that area do for that church will do them little good. A church needs to do things for itself and by itself. The indigenous princi-

---

18. Ibid. p. 125.
19. The early efforts at planting the church were one long evangelistic meeting.
20. Yamamori and Lawson, *Intro. Church Growth*, p. 134.
21. Melvin L. Hodges, *The Indigenous Church*, (Springfield, Missouri: Gospel Publishing House, 1953).

ple demands self-supporting, self-governing, self-propagating churches. The paid leadership of the church becomes less and less necessary because of the church people being involved in the ministry to the community.

It is nothing short of remarkable how quickly Paul turned churches over to their own leadership. His longest ministry was a little over two years at Ephesus. Churches were begun, leadership ordained, and he moved on. These churches were comprised of local people. Sometimes others were sent to deal with their problems. Such people as Timothy or Titus visited the churches establishing and strengthening them.

12. GOOD AND BIBLICAL, THEN BIG.

Much in the realm of super-churchism today tends toward quantity of people, not quality of commitment. This appears to be in direct violation of many scriptural teachings. Hebrews 8:5 " 'See,' He says, 'that you make all things according to the pattern which was shown you on the mountain.' " The primary illustration is given about Moses. The direct application has reference to the church. II Timothy 1:13 advises us to, "Retain the standard of sound words. . . ." Titus was told, "But as for you, speak the things which are fitting for sound doctrine," Titus 2:1. Paul warned the Galatians, "But even though we, or an angel from heaven, should preach to you a gospel contrary to that which we have preached to you, let him be accursed," Galatians 1:8. When we begin to modify the gospel to fit the thinking of our day or to permit some person into the church who refuses to submit to scriptural teachings, we soon rob the gospel of its validity. Where will this compromise of truth end?

The writer is acquainted with one church in a small town that grew from 125 people in the process of about a year and a half, to over 850 people in attendance. The following year the church went back to about seventy-five people in attendance with an indebtedness of nearly one half million dollars. The principle was big first, then good later. The church had not been founded in good, Biblical teaching, but on the giving away of gifts, gimmicks, motorcycles, and prizes for those who were best in bringing other people into the church. Those who can get the bus the fullest are heroes. Such theatrical gimmicks have been used as having the preacher sit on top of the church building and eat a chicken dinner. But this is not founded in and upon the word of God. Church growth advocates should not be interested in something being big unless it is first good. Our purpose is to build a church that is founded in and upon the teachings of Jesus Christ and His apostles where every member has a personal relationship with Jesus Christ. This is the principle of being good and Biblical first, then big. If the church is first good, then it should grow big and be a blessing to the community and all who come in contact with it.

All the preceding principles should be studied and incorporated into the life of the church because they have been demonstrated to be sources of quality church growth.

Chapter 3 Examination

1. Explain in a few words the church growth principle called, "Koinonia."

2. What is religious relativism and what has it done for the church?

3. Explain briefly what a people movement is. What can we learn from this principle?

4. What do social structures have to do with church growth?

5. How can we close the back door of the church?

6. What does church policy have to do with church growth?

7. What do we mean by the psychology of expectancy and church growth?

8. What part does the Holy Spirit have in church growth?

9. How does individual witness apply to a growing church?

10. Why should Christians need revival?

11. What is the indigenous principle of church growth?

12. Explain why big does not necessarily mean that a church is good.

4

SYSTEMS ANALYSIS AND THREE TYPES OF CHURCH GROWTH

". . . 'see,' he says, 'that you make all things according to the pattern that was shown you. . . .' " Hebrews 8:5

It would be impossible to divide all churches into three different classes or systems, yet for the sake of analysis, it might be helpful if we could examine a chart produced by Dr. Steven A. Hancock.[1] His chart shows three systems or types of church operation. He has shown the *predominating* procedures of these types of churches and has divided them into System I, II, and III types of operations. Under each system he lists four categories of characteristics. We will look at three of these four categories: diagnosis, programming, and product.

SYSTEM I

The System I church diagnosis shows an ignorance problem. Each of the three systems sees the need for teaching. Dr. Hancock suggests

---

1. Dr. Stephen Hancock, "Systems of Church Operation" charts, see charts on following pages of this work. (The chart has been slightly revised.)

that the System I church would view proper treatment as more indoctrination, training, inspiration, Word-to-life experience. If we could just do a better job of teaching everything would be all right, is the philosophy. The strategy of this particular church is to continue essentially on its present course, work harder, add more programming, and better supervision.

The success of the System I church is measured by how the people feel about their church, its leadership, and its programming. Spiritual growth is measured by the interest, attendance at meetings, and a dedication to the things that are being done in the church. The Sunday services, in the building, are unconsciously felt to be the climax of all that is done within this type of church. If there is a big attendance, they have a good church. The preacher or the clergyman is the gatekeeper and the lead worker and he puts on a performance for those who attend. The elders of the church are a board of directors, directing primarily the activities of the preacher. Their job is felt to be keeping the preacher in line. The people, or laymen, support the church so the preacher can go about his duties. As long as they give their money and attend regularly, they feel they are doing their part.

The programming of this particular type of church shows control to be semi-direct. The supervision of everything is under the direction of the preacher who promotes, exhorts, and checks up on what is going on in the church. If things go well, he is a good guy, if not, he is the bad guy. The organization of the church is highly structured with a continual need for housekeeping. More organization is viewed as the cure-all for most problems.

The motivation is emotional "ought-to" manipulation of the people to get them to do the things that the leadership feels they "ought to" do. If the people do not do as the leader wants, they are made to feel guilty.

The meetings are large group rituals, impersonal, structure centered, people passive, and often do not really meet the needs of the people. People are spectators rather than participants. Decisions are made by the preacher, through the officers, to the people who ratify the things that have been done from the top of the organization.

Change is brought about by political action within the life of the church through the church board, or campaigns led by the preacher, an elder or deacon. The sales approach is the method of evangelism used. Virtually all evangelism is programmed by the church. It is not felt that evangelism is the average member's responsibility. Most converts are won by the salaried staff. The ministry is what we might call indirect.

The products of this type of church do not nearly reach its potential. The total percentage of functioning ministers within the body is at best 10-15 percent of the total membership. This greatly hampers the possibilities of growth within the church body and does not represent the New Testament ideal.[2] The conversions within such a body might be dozens to hundreds, but usually are very limited in number. There may be none. Reversions to the old way of life by the converts going back to the world, are from 70-90 percent. This is caused in part by lack of careful discipleship and integration into ministry. Attendance change might show positive growth of as much as 10 percent annually. Tithing families within this particular type of church comprise from 5-20 percent of the total attending members.

The majority of churches today are System I type churches. This approach to evangelism is one of the reasons why churches are either growing slowly or not at all. They are *hiring* a person to do their work. A church is robbed of its power and potential by such programming.

SYSTEM II

The second type of church is identified, for the sake of analysis, as a System II church. The problem with this type of church is seen as volitional. How can the church grow? What must be done to build the church? How can we get it moving? The treatment is thought to be indoctrination. The law is laid down; people are confronted and are inspired. The theory is that people need to be taught. If enough teaching takes place, they will automatically take their place.

The strategy is to develop super-aggressive members committed to confrontational evangelism. People are almost coerced into conforming to the leader's evangelization program. The success in the life of the church is measured by attendance increase. If there is a modest or large increase in the number in the public assembly, the church is considered strong — a good, healthy church. The problem with this thinking is that the people still may be conforming out of improper motives and not be

---

2. Ephesians 4:11-12.

changed into the image of Christ. Attendance says something, but is not a sufficient gauge to check the quality of a church's programming.

The spiritual growth of the people is marked by conforming behavior. While conforming to the likeness of the church leaders may be desirable, this behavior must come from proper motives and principles. If it does not, problems later are inevitable. Yet, behavior is directed to a modeling of the status quo of the church and its leader, not Christ. The proper ideal is to grow to Christ-likeness.

The culmination is seen as being Sunday in the church building. This thinking robs the church of its greatest opportunity to minister in the community. The culmination should come when the whole congregation is dispersed into the community to minister for Christ.

The preacher or clergyman is the gatekeeper, church director, and the leader. The elders are the preacher's men who learn to say "yes" when the preacher speaks. If they do not go along with what is being said by the preacher, they are replaced. The people are laymen who support the preacher in everything he does, and if they do not support what he is doing then they can go somewhere else. This type of church is distinguishable by its heavy-handed leadership. One either conforms or seeks another church.

The programming of the church is with direct control over everything in the whole life of the church by the preacher-manager-overseer-pastor of that church. What he says is law. Supervision is by promotion, exhortation, checks and confrontation for those who do not measure up to what is expected. The organization of this type of church is highly structured evangelism with many involved in going out and reproducing themselves spiritually, and bringing other people into the church.

The motivation is again emotional "ought-to" manipulation or confrontation, "This is your duty and you ought to do it in order to conform to the life that is expected by the preacher of the church." If people do not conform they may be put out of office or coerced either by direct or subtle means.

The meetings are large group, ritual type, personally orchestrated meetings, with passive people. The people are spectators at a public performance. The people are not involved, not even as much as at a ball game or sporting event. The people have little to say about the direction the church will take.

The decisions are dictated by the preacher, who relays them to the officers of the church, and then on to the people. The programming could be styled "heavy-handed." Change is brought about by coercion.

Evangelism is again the sales approach, most programmed by the church. The candidate for conversion is grabbed by the lapel of his coat and asked, "Have you been born again?" This may take place on the street, bus or plane. While it is not bad to talk to one about Christ anywhere, more is needed than just a quick or passing, "Do you believe in Jesus?" type approach. Most converts are won by paid staff, church leaders, or Sunday School teachers, and members within the church. The ministry is what we might call semi-direct, but not yet as it could be. This church is an improvement over a Systems I church in many ways.

When we talk about the products of such a church, 10-20 percent of the members are functioning ministers. Conversions may be dozens to thousands. Reversions back to the world (people going out the back door of the church) are from 80-90 percent of those won. Such a church will report hundreds of baptisms each year while only posting an attendance gain of 10-20 percent of that number. What happens to the 80 percent who do not stay? What does II Peter 2:21 mean if it is not talking about such a matter: "For it would be better for them not to have known the way of righteousness, than having known it, to turn away from the holy commandment delivered to them." Attendance change in the life of the church is from 10-30 percent. Tithing families usually comprise about 10-30 percent of the total people in attendance. This particular System II type of church is demonstrated by large, super-churches of today. You'll find them among several denominational groups. This system shows some signs that are possibly more encouraging than a System I type church, but still is not fully in keeping with the principles laid down in the New Testament. The System II church does not explain the great growth that took place in the New Testament Church in the book of Acts.

SYSTEM III

The System III type of church starts out with a diagnosis of a volitional problem; that is, how to get the individual membership of the church moving to do the work that Christ called the church to do: "Go therefore and made disciples of all the nations. . . ."[3] This is recognized as being entirely too large a job for a few to accomplish. Only when the teaching of Ephesians 4:11-12 is implemented can there be a hope to accomplish the task. When it can be said, as it was in Acts 8:4, "They went everywhere preaching the word," it will be done. How can we accomplish this great task?

The treatment is seen in a different light than either of the other two types of churches. It is shown to be instruction in the grace of God and support given from life-to-life. It is a discipling process — the gospel being taught from one who has learned it to another, and then on to another who will teach another, moving from life to life, example to example. Jesus' command was to "make disciples." The Greek word *mathetes* means "a learner (from *manthano*, to learn, from a root *math-*, indicating thought accompanied by endeavor). . . ."[4] Here is the crucial area of difference. People are led to Christ and then discipled till they are able to disciple another. While each system sees the need for teaching, the System III church sees teaching plus involvement of every member in ministry as the crying need. The goal is the discipling by one member leading another person to do the things that the discipler has learned.

There are many different authors who would advocate this type of treatment. One very fine book on this subject is *Disciples Are Made — Not Born*,[5] by Walter A. Henrichsen. The author advocates that a church ought to be a discipling institution in which a person who becomes a Christian adopts the life style of Jesus Christ, and the person who has discipled him, and who in turn will disciple another person. The strategy is to disciple all persons to be like Christ. This certainly goes back to the principle that made the New Testament Church so vital in its life and successful in the Roman world in which it was born.

Spiritual growth is shown in the life by Christ-like behavior. It grows out of Christ-like motives in the lives of people as they truly adopt the life-style of Jesus, Himself, not the life-style of the preacher or church leaders. "Until we all attain to the unity of the faith, and of the

---

3. Matthew 28:19
4. W. E. Vine, *Expository Dictionary of New Testament Words*, (Westwood, New Jersey: Fleming H. Revell Company, 1958) p. 316.
5. Walter A. Henrichsen, *Disciples Are Made — Not Born*, (Wheaton, Illinois: SP Publications, Inc., 1974).

knowledge of the Son of God, to a mature man, to the measure of the stature which belongs to the fullness of Christ."[6] There is plenty of room for growth in all members of the body.

The climax in this particular type of church is in the daily life where the person recognizes that to be a Christian means to be daily in every way following the example of Jesus, the Master discipler. In whatever they do, in word or in deed, they do all to the glory of God.[7] Their whole life is a ministry to Christ and an opportunity to serve Him.

The whole week offers many opportunities to minister for Christ in their own realm of work and influence. The preacher is viewed as an enabler, an equipper, a trainer, a model of behavior in the likeness of Jesus Christ. The elders of this type of church are shepherds, servants, counselors, overseers and instructors. The people are all ministers instead of having just one minister in the church. The church thus expands its workers to nearly 100 percent of the body. Every person is recognized as having a special gift and ministry for Christ.[8] Each person is helped to recognize and use their gifts for the kingdom.

The programming of such a System III type church shows that the control is indirect. No one is doing something because they have to do so or because they are coerced to do so, but are doing so because they want to, because they have the privilege of ministry.

Supervision is along the lines of modeling, sharing, supporting, and teaching. Some confrontation and encouragement to do the things that Christ has said to do does take place.

The organization is limited and simple, according to the New Testament plan. Evangelism and ministry are considered to be the very purposes and goals of the organization of the church.

The motivation to do what is right comes from conscience, and invitation to do so, and some confrontation. Through teaching and modeling, the person is led to follow the life-style of the model and Jesus.

Meetings consist of large groups, small groups, pairs, families, one to one, process centered, personal, open, with people actively involved. There are large groups, but this is only one of a variety of methods used to communicate the teaching and life-style of Jesus. Jesus, Lord of

---

6. Ephesians 4:13.
7. Colossians 3:17.
8. Ephesians 4:7-8.

glory, took time for one person or small groups. These few, adopting His style changed the world. People can come and share not only their insights but their needs in an atmosphere of love and warmth.

Decisions are made by a consensus throughout the body of the church. Heavy-handedness is gone, there is much openness. People get used to expressing their ideas and feelings openly. After the body is informed and has an opportunity to express their feelings, decisions are made.

Change is brought about by study groups seeking the scriptures and doing what the Bible teaches. The Bible is the standard and rule of faith and practice. The appeal is: what did Jesus teach? What does the Bible say? Evangelism is that of a study approach where people are carefully taught.[9] Most converts are discipled by people within the church who are unsalaried ministers within the body, leading others, who upon independent investigation and initiative, choose to be doing this work.

As we talk about the products of the System III type of church, we find that from 70-90 percent of the people are functioning ministers. Conversions are from dozens to hundreds; reversions to the world are from 10-30 percent. Attendance change shows growth to be from 10-100 percent per year. Tithing families within such a body are from 70-90 percent of those attending. They are freely giving at least a tithe or more to the work of the kingdom. They recognize this as a part of their ministry and service.

There are many advocates for this System III type of church and the author is one of these. We must work towards a New Testament Church, centered in the mutual ministry of equipped people who are serving Jesus Christ. It would be impossible to divide all the churches into three different categories, but the principle is well demonstrated that many churches fall somewhere near one of these three different types.

There appear to be too few System III type churches whose aim and goal is to train every member in the body to be a minister for Christ helping reclaim all of creation, especially that segment of creation within which he lives and with which only he comes in contact daily, for the Lord of glory. It is the hope of the author that the reader will seek to become a living, active disciple for Jesus Christ, submitting his very life-style and way of thinking to the way of the Master, Jesus Christ.

---

9. See Chapter 11.

CHECKING SCRIPTURE

Let us now take a more careful look at the Systems Analysis Chart with a view of seeing what scriptural principles are practiced or violated. We will do so by comparing the Systems I, II, & III practices.

PERSPECTIVE

The Systems I church diagnoses the problem as *ignorance* while the Systems II & III churches see the problem as *volitional*. It is true that the gospel must be taught, but to teach without practice brings a sort of spiritual constipation and lethargy. The Bible says, "teaching them to *observe* all that I commanded you;" Matthew 28:20. Ephesians 4:11-12, ". . . *teachers*, for the equipping of the saints *for the work of service* to the building up of the body of Christ." We must couple teaching and doing.

The *strategy* of the three types of churches is quite different. The Systems I churches working harder while following a wrong course will never solve the problem. The Systems II church's idea is a bit better yet not really what the Bible teaches. The Systems III church's goal is well stated in Ephesians 4:13, "until we all attain to the unity of the faith, and of the knowledge of the Son of God, to a mature man, to the measure of the stature which belongs to the fullness of Christ." The Systems III plan is to help people grow to be like Christ.

The *success* of the three types of churches is quite different. A positive attitude towards leadership or attendance increases cannot be an adequate measure of success for the church. If so, the lodge or winning ball teams would qualify as successful churches. Success of a Christian can only be measured by their Christ-likeness. ". . . Christ in you the hope of glory," Colossians 1:27.

The perspective of the three types of churches on the *eldership* is very different. In the Systems I church the elders rule over the preacher. In the Systems II church the preacher rules over the elders. The Bible says, "*Shepherd* the flock of God among you, not under compulsion, but voluntarily, according to the will of God; and not for sordid gain, but with eagerness; nor yet as *lording it over* those allotted to your charge, but proving to be examples to the flock," I Peter 5:2-3. There is no

57

SYSTEMS OF CHURCH OPERATION
Predominating Procedures

		SYSTEM I	SYSTEM II	SYSTEM III
PERSPECTIVE	Diagnosis:	Ignorance problem.	Volitional Problem.	Volitional Problem.
	Treatment:	Indoctrination, training, inspiration . . . Word-to-life.	Indoctrination, (law), confrontation, inspiration . . .	Instruction (grace), support . . . Life-to-life.
	Strategy:	Continue essentially on the present course, but work harder and add more programming and better supervision.	Develop super-aggressive members committed to confrontation evangelism.	Disciple all persons to be like Christ.
	Success:	People feeling a positive regard toward church leadership and programming.	Attendance increase.	Evident change toward Christ-likeness in lives of people.
	Spiritual Growth:	Interest, attendance at meetings, esprit de corps.	Conforming behavior.	Christ-like behavior growing out of Christ-like motives.
	Climax:	Sunday-in-the-building.	Sunday-in-the-building.	Daily life.
	Preacher:	Clergyman, gatekeeper, lead worker.	Clergyman, the ideal, gatekeeper, church director.	Enabler, coach, equipper, model.
	Elders:	Board of directors.	Preacher's men.	Shepherds, servants, counselors, instructors, overseers.
	People:	Laymen who support the church.	Laymen who support the preacher.	Ministers.
PROGRAMMING	Control:	Semi-Direct.	Direct.	Indirect.
	Supervision:	Promotion, exhortation and checks.	Promotion, exhortation, checks, confrontation.	Modeling, sharing, supporting, confrontation.
	Organization:	Highly structured . . . housekeeping.	Highly structured . . . evangelism.	Simple, limited . . . evangelism and ministry.
	Motivation:	Emotional, "ought," manipulation.	Emotional, "ought," manipulation, confrontation.	Conscience, "invitation," confrontation.

58

PROGRAMMING cont.	Meetings:	Large group, ritual, impersonal, structure-centered. People-passive.	Large group, ritual, impersonal, orchestrated. People-passive.	Large group, small group, pair, family. Process-centered, personal, open. People active.
	Decisions:	Preacher through officers to people, who ratify. Political.	Preacher to officers and people.	Consensus.
	Change:		Coerced.	Group study.
	Evangelism:	Sales approach. Virtually all programmed by the church.	Sales approach. Majority programmed by the church. Most converts won by salaried staff.	Study approach. Most converts discipled by unsalaried leaders upon independent initiative.
	Ministry:	Indirect.	Semi-direct.	Direct.
PRODUCT	Functioning Ministers:	10-15 percent	10-20 percent	70-90 percent
	Conversions:	Dozens to hundreds	Dozens to thousands	Dozens to hundreds
	Reversions:	70-90 percent	80-90 percent	10-30 percent
	Attendance Change:	0-10 percent + –	10-30 percent +	10-100 percent +
	Tithing Families:	5-20 percent	10-30 percent	70-90 percent
PROPONENTS	Preachers:	Vast majority	Jack Hyles, Jerry Falwell, John Rawlings	John MacArthur, Jr., Ray Stedman, Robert Girard, Carl Ketcherside.
	Professors:	Vast majority	Elmer Towns	Larry Richards, Findley Edge, Gene Getz.
	Churches:	Vast majority	FBC, Hammond, IN,[1] Thomas Road Baptist Church,[2] Lynchburg, VA	Fellowship Bible Church, Dallas, TX,[3] Belmont Church of Christ, Nashville, TN[4]

1. Elmer Towns, *World's Largest Sunday School*, 1974.
2. Elmer Towns, *Church Aflame*, 1971.
3. Kay Oliver, "Fellowship Plus," *Moody Monthly*, January, 1975, pp. 36-39.
4. Victor Hunter, "Openness and Growth: The Belmont Experience," *Mission*, March, 1973, pp. 17-22.

place for heavy-handed domination but rather working together in love.

PROGRAMMING

Next, consider the programming of the three types of churches. One of the key areas of the church is its *meetings*. In the Systems I and II church a lot of emphasis is placed on largeness. In a Systems III church there are large meetings but more emphasis is placed on a variety of meetings and especially on small groups and pairs. Is this a scriptural emphasis? Yes. Remember the ministry of Jesus. He spent His best hours with twelve. Jesus took time for Zacchaeus, the woman at the well, Nicodemus and others. Paul preached "publicly and from house to house." Acts 20:20. The "house church" is repeatedly mentioned in Acts and the Epistles.

Consider the matter of *decision making* in the church. The Systems III church places more emphasis on taking time to listen. In the Jerusalem Church, when a problem arose, a congregational meeting was called. "And the twelve summoned the congregation of the disciples and said, . . ." Acts 6:2. The congregation was asked to submit names of people who could be set over the business to solve the problem. There was no heavy-handedness. In another place the elders are warned to not lord over those allotted in their charge, I Peter 5:3. In actual practice, open lines of communication will solve most problems before they become serious ones.

In the Systems III church there are a remarkable number of people involved in direct *ministry*. In the author's church, during a thirteen week period, forty-nine people came to accept Christ. Forty-eight were taught and led by church members. This was true in the New Testament Church. Both Philip and Steven were out preaching and soul winning, Acts chapter 6,7 & 8. At Damascus it was said, "Now there was a certain disciple at Damascus, named Ananias. . . ." Acts 9:10. He was the soul winner. Priscilla and Aquila were out preaching and teaching. In the privacy of their home they met with Apollos and taught him the way of God more adequately, Acts 18:24-19:5. Unless the ministry in our churches is direct and carried on by the full membership the church cannot be the dynamic force intended by Christ.

PRODUCT

Look briefly at the section of the chart called "Product". In a Systems I & II church only a limited number of people actually get involved in front line *ministry*. In the Systems III church possibly 70-90 percent become involved. This difference is not easily achieved in the Systems III church. Without a doubt this was Christ's plan for the church. It is inherent in His marching orders, "Go therefore and make *disciples of all* the nations, baptizing them in the name of the Father and the Son and the Holy Spirit, *teaching them to observe all* that I commanded you;..." Matthew 28:19-20. We will learn in Chapter V that a disciple is a doing-learner. Right in this text He commands us all to go make disciples. By the example of the over fifty disciples Paul mentions in his writings we can be sure that both men and women were involved in this work of ministry. This emphasis supplies the workers Christ prayed for, Luke 10:2. "And He was saying to them, 'the harvest is plentiful, but the laborers are few; therefore beseech the Lord of the harvest to send out laborers into His harvest.' "

Another encouraging product of the Systems III church is the small number of reversions to the world. There are several causes of this. When a preacher and a few elders do all the soul winning they do not have time to maintain a close relationship with the new convert. This is not true when everyone is involved. When people help lead their friends to Christ they continue to be their friends and a part of their social life.

Finally, another refreshing spin-off is what this teaching does for the finances of the church. People who really get involved in the church work will support it with their money. In the author's church, offerings increased 644 percent in just four years.

Won't you give serious consideration to your church's predominating procedures? Restoring the Biblical plan of operation can bring tremendous vitality to Christ's body today. A plan of discipleship will be suggested in Chapters 5 and 21. Remember, our efforts are useless unless undergirded with prayer.

SYSTEMS OF CHURCH OPERATION CHART:
AN EXPLANATION

The Author Is Not Saying...	*The Author Is Saying...*
All three systems have equal scriptural support.	One system has more scriptural support than do the other two.
Churches are consistently, 100% either System I, II or III.	Churches tend to be a mixture of two or three systems.
This is an evaluation of the spirituality of the churches.	This is a description of the ways churches are actually functioning.
The chart is final, complete, perfect and unbiased.	This is a starting point to help leaders develop and clarify their understanding of the N.T. model.
The chart is based on hard statistical evidence.	The basis is personal church experience, careful observation, training under recognized leaders in all three church systems.
Represents a developmental order in a series of three phases.	Churches plan to move from left to right but seldom in the reverse.
Most churches have consciously chosen to be either I, II or III.	Most churches are hardly aware of the extent of the options described on this chart.
This represents what a church necessarily preaches or professes.	This describes what churches do and achieve viz. functional theology (Titus 1:16)
Churches in any system will act only as described.	These are predominating procedures, i.e. what is done 51% + of the time or in a crisis.
Represents the worst of some systems and the best of another.	The chart represents the common predominating procedures in each system.
These systems function only in the non-Restoration Movement, evangelical world.	Each system has Restoration churches that defend it as the accurate expression of N.T. Christianity.
Most leaders disagree concerning which is the N.T. ideal.	There is wide agreement concerning which is the N.T. ideal.
Most leaders will not be able to see a major gap between the N.T. model and their present practice.	Most eventually agree that their church is operating with one of the less desirable systems.
Any one not agreeing with the author is not a N.T. Christian.	N.T. Christians may disagree concerning the ideal N.T. model and the present practices of the church.

CENTERING CHURCH OPERATION

Extreme	Balance	Extreme

Churches today need to move away from the extremes of present practice in certain areas of church operation to a more centered position. A clue to normalizing operations in local church ministry involves practicing a balance among the variety of possible approaches or seeking the mid-point between possible extremes. This is the New Testament orientation and precedent in church operation.

	Common Extreme[A]	System III Balance[B]	Uncommon Extreme[C]
Buildings	Shrine	Shelter	Sin
Groupings	Large Group	Variety[D]	Independent
Communications	Monologue	Variety[E]	Activity
Mental Appeal	Rational	Holistic	Emotional
Participation	Passive	Combination	Active
Fellowship	Impersonal	Intimate	Invading
Change	Conservation	Improvement	Novelty
Methodology	Traditional	Effective	Iconoclastic
Structure	Extensive	Limited	Eliminated
Programming	Uniform	Mutli-level	Individualized
Elders	Popes or Passers	Pastors	Pariahs
Preacher	Controller	Servant-leader	Follower

A. Dominant practice in churches today.
B. Most desirable practice.
C. Radical alternative.
D. Independent, large group, small group, pair, family, inter-congregational.
E. Monologue, dialogue, group process, media, activity, non-verbal.

Chapter 4 Examination

1. What is the diagnosis of what is wrong in a Systems I, Systems II and System III church?

2. Explain the difference between the strategy of the Systems I, II, III church.

3. What is the elder's place in a System I, II and III church?

4. In the programming of a System I, II and III church, what distinguishes the System III church's meetings from the other two?

5. Is the author trying to say that all churches fall entirely into a clear Systems I, II or III category?

6. The Greek word *mathetes* means what?

7. Name two preachers who advocate a Systems II type church.

8. In a Systems III church, decisions come from_____
_____. How is this reached?

9. Explain how most converts are won in a system III church.

10. In a Systems III church, the climax of all that is done is seen when?

5

DISCIPLESHIP

1. UNDERSTANDING THE WORD

> Go therefore and make disciples of all the nations, baptizing them in the name of the Father and the Son and the Holy Spirit, teaching them to observe all that I commanded you; and lo, I am with you always, even to the end of the age.[1]

This passage of scripture is one of the most familiar to Christian people in the whole Bible and yet it is probably misunderstood by most people. The area of difficulty lies with the word "discipleship." A disciple is said to be "a learner." That is only part of the truth. An in-depth study of this word is imperative today.

> But to each one of us grace was given according to the measure of Christ's gift. Therefore it says, "when He ascended on high, He led captive a host of captives, and He gave gifts to men." Now this expression, "He ascend-

---

1. Matthew 28:19-20.

ed," what does it mean except that He also had descended into the lower parts of the earth? He who descended is Himself also He who ascended far above all the heavens, that he might fill all things. And he gave some as apostles, and some as prophets, and some as evangelists, and some as pastors and teachers, for the equipping of the saints for the work of service, to the building up of the body of Christ;[2]

This passage of scripture is also very familiar among the Christian community, while at the same time it is often with little understanding. There are several things that will help to clear up the meaning. Verse 7 says "grace was given according to the measure of Christ's gift." Each Christian person is gifted by Christ in a special way to work in service to the Lord in discipleship. Verse 8 says "he gave gifts to men." Every Christian person is gifted for service or discipleship within the body of Christ.

Many people are unwilling to be involved in discipleship because of sacrifices expected. Paul speaks of Christ ascending but before he ascended he had to descend into the lower parts of the earth. What is meant? It is true of all discipleship that one will not serve well until he has first been willing to condescend. He must be willing to become a nobody, to be involved in things that seem of little consequence, to serve in insignificant ways, and to grow in his ministry. As he descends, he is prepared to ascend to greater service in the body of Christ. Finally, all of the various giftedness within the body is for the equipping of saints for the work of service or ministry so that Christ's body can be built up.

And the things which you have heard from me in the presence of many witnesses, these entrust to faithful men, who will be able to teach others also.[3]

An old principle of discipleship is laid down. This principle is the expansion of workers, one training another who trains another who trains another to an ever expanding pyramid. This is the basic principle of discipleship.

But you followed my teachings, conduct, purpose, faith, patience, love, perseverance, persecutions, sufferings, such as happened to me at An-

---

2. Ephesians 4:7-12.
3. II Timothy 2:2.

tioch, at Iconium and at Lystra; what persecutions I endured, and out of them all the Lord delivered me![4]

Let's go back and talk a little bit about misunderstanding. In our present world our children are quick to use all sorts of terms which they often do not understand. These terms, whether sex terms or psychological terms, are applied with freedom to their friends and acquaintances. These terms are often very grossly misunderstood. The children are embarrassed when they find out the true meaning of the words that they have been using. This is also true in the church world today. The misunderstanding of several key words in the scriptures have led to unbiblical practices that have hurt the church.

Let's talk about the historical setting of the problem. Originally twelve men, the apostles of Christ, won an estimated 25% of the world to Christ in about sixty years. The gospel was preached by them as far away as India, possibly in China, Africa, and maybe as far away as Europe and England.

By the time of Emperor Constantine some etsimate that 50% to 75% of the world was won to Christ. By anyone's standards these are remarkable examples of church growth. Wouldn't it be wonderful to know their methodology? We can know their methodology from a study of scripture and understanding of one Biblical word.

Let's examine three religious movements in America to see what has happened from 1900 until 1986. In the year 1900 these three movements each had about one million members. They are the Southern Baptists, the Utah branch Mormons and the Christian Churches or Churches of Christ. By present estimates the Southern Baptists now have approximately sixteen million members (this is probably over-enthusiastic), the Latter-day Saints claim 5.2 million, and the Christian Church (Independent) boasts an amazing 1,300,000 (amazing due to their lack of growth). These estimates were made by Dr. Max Ward Randall of Lincoln Christian Seminary. His estimates were based on the *Directory of the Ministry of the Church of Christ and Christian Churches*.

Let's use the latter of these churches as an example. Of their some 5,600 churches, one author said that nearly half the churches had not

---

4. II Timothy 3:10-11.

won anyone to Christ in the course of a year. They could best be described as dead, indifferent, weak, or dying churches. This is not very encouraging.

Looking at Christianity as a whole is also perplexing. Are we really gaining on the world's population? Most totals of membership seem to indicate that Christianity is losing out to other religions such as Islam, Buddhism, or Humanism.

Some of the cults have recaptured the Biblical discipleship but on a false doctrinal base. These groups seem to be showing remarkable numerical growth. In spite of the combined efforts of all different groups called Christian people, of the over four billion people on the face of the earth, it is estimated that less than one billion of them are devoted to Christianity of any kind. Most religious people would not be willing to include all of these people as true Christians. Christianity needs some major revisions of policy if we are to again take the world.

The problem in part is a misunderstood word. The key word is the word "disciple." The Greek word is *mathetes*. What does the word actually mean? We have been taught for years that a disciple is a learner. That is only part of the meaning and as with most half-truths, it is very dangerous to the cause of Christ. It is a much more powerful word than that. Good teaching and learning are important, but are not nearly enough. The crux of our problem today is the misunderstanding of this great word.

Since churches fail to comprehend this great word, they wrongly direct their efforts in trying to solve the church's problems. Many churches feel that if they could do a better job of teaching, everything would be okay. It is true that there are facts to be taught, but that is not enough. The problem will only be solved when we fathom properly the word "disciple." What does the word mean? The Hebrew word, *talmid*, which is a synonym of the Greek word, *mathetes*, meant to master the Torah, or the first five books of the Bible. Along with mastering and teaching the Torah, the father taught his son three other things, a trade, to swim, and to choose a wife. The Hebrew word simply meant to master information; the Greek word has an expanded meaning.

The word "disciple" in Greek meant thought plus action. Not only were the learners taught, but they did. They adopted the lifestyle of the discipler. To be a disciple of Jesus meant that one was stamped into the very likeness of Christ.

Several illustrations could be given to show the meaning of this word. A disciple was an apprentice, a doctor in training, with a trained physician in the background watching as he performed the skills that he had been studying. Or a musician could be used as an example. Not only did he study the notes of the scale, but he was taught while playing the instrument under supervision. The word has a sense of personal attachment to another person. This personal attachment changed and shaped the entire lifestyle of the one being discipled. There could be no doubt as to who was exerting the influence and the formative powers, it was the discipler upon the disciple. The disciple always accepted unconditionally the discipler's authority. This master discipler for the Christian of course is Christ.

Jesus loved and used this word often. It was a part of His everyday speech. He spoke of His intimate relationship with His followers. They were repeatedly called His disciples. This was true until the Crucifixion, after which He suddenly stopped using this word. Why? The disciples' actions ceased to be those of disciples. They no longer were following the lifestyle of Jesus. In fact they had gone back to their own way and to their old jobs.

The word was taken up again after they were recalled to discipleship. Not until Acts 6:1 were they again called disciples.

Let's examine the characteristics of a Biblical disciple and show what re-establishing the significance of this Biblical word can mean to the life of the church. The Biblical usage shows these characteristics of a disciple.

The commitment of a person's whole being to another person. In Luke 5:1-11 Jesus performed His first miraculous draught of fishes. At that time the disciples left everything and followed Him. In John 1:45 other men who came to be His disciples said that "we have found Him. . . ." In Luke 5:27, Jesus in calling His disciples said, "Follow Me." The rich young ruler was not accepted as a disciple because he was unwilling to leave what he had and follow Jesus.

Another characteristic of a Biblical disciple was obedience. Jesus taught His disciples that "a slave is not greater than his master,"[5] indicating that they needed to be subject to him in all ways. Slaves had

---

5. John 13:16.

69

few rights. Jesus taught His disciples, "a disciple was not above the teacher."[6] Teachers had considerably more authority than in our day. Therefore submission was expected. In Mark 11:1 Jesus gives orders to His disciples as He sends them to get the ass colt for the triumphal entry. At a later point in the book, Mark 14:12, He sent two to get the room for the Passover. They were ready to be obedient to Him.

Another characteristic of the disciple was his willingness to suffer. A Christian said that he had a dream in which he approached Heaven and was met by a little baldheaded man who asked him if he had any scars. The Christian was surprised at the question, and asked what the meaning of all this was. He repeated the question to the approaching Christian, "Do you have any scars?" At this point the little man explained to him that "those who live Godly in Christ Jesus shall suffer persecution." He wanted to see what kind of scars he received in the course of serving the Lord. The disciple had to be willing to suffer. Jesus promised His disciples that they would be "as sheep in the midst of wolves; . . . they will deliver you up to the courts, and scourge you in their synagogues; . . . for my sake."[7] In John 15:18 He warned His disciples that they would be hated. In John 16:1-3 they were cautioned that they would be treated as outcasts, and those who would kill them would think they had actually done God a favor. Discipleship demands suffering and sacrifice.

Another characteristic of the disciple was that he bore testimony or witness to a person. Jesus said, "You are witnesses of these things."[8] Their job was to go out and bear witness to that which they *had seen.* "You shall be My witnesses."[9] John was an eyewitness of Jesus (John 19:35). "The disciple who bears witness of Jesus,"[10] of course was John. Active discipleship today must bear testimony to Jesus, not to some church or organization or program within the church.

And finally, a disciple was to learn and to do. According to the teachings of the Great Commission, all Christians are disciples or not Christians at all. All Christian disciples will become not only disciples but

---

6. Matthew 10:24.
7. Matthew 10:16-18.
8. Luke 24:44-48.
9. Acts 1:8.
10. John 21:24.

disciplers of others as they go on in the never ending process of expanding the work of the kingdom.

2. WHAT THIS PROPER UNDERSTANDING CAN MEAN TO THE CHURCH.

What the church needs today is not to think big but to think small, because real church growth comes from nutrition not addition. Bodily health comes from taking care of the details. When the body is healthy from within there will be new birth, and out of the new birth, growth will come. The main problem with the church today is that the body is ill and cannot grow because of this illness. A proper understanding of this word "discipleship" will bring Christians to recognize that they are to learn and do. The Great Commission takes on a greatly expanded meaning, "make disciples of all the nations."[11]

Discipleship has been a great blessing to the work of Christ in the churches in which the author has served. On one Sunday there were four different men out preaching somewhere who came out of this discipleship program. It is a process of learning and doing.

The second great benefit of understanding this word in the church today is that every Christian will begin to use his gifts.[12] Every Christian has been gifted, every Christian has a special talent to offer to bring health to the body. Understanding the proper meaning of discipleship helps people begin to use their gifts for the building up of the body of the church.

A proper understanding of this word will greatly expand the witness of the church.[13] The disciple will teach others and make them disciples, who will teach others and make them disciples, in an ever expanding circle of witnessing for Christ. Finally, this will make the church again a great dynamic force for good to people and to the world.

Discipleship is something in which every Christian is to be involved. Discipleship can bring happiness to Christians. Discipleship involves three things in the author's church. Bible study, by the disciple and

---

11. Matthew 28:19.
12. Ephesians 4:7-12.
13. II Timothy 2:2.

discipler, regular prayer with daily devotions, and finally outreach to ministry for the body of Christ.

Efforts in discipleship must continue until we grow to the measure of the stature which belongs to the fullness of Christ.[14] To become like the master discipler, Jesus, should be the goal of every Christian.

High in the white hills of New Hampshire a great stone face was formed by nature on the perpendicular side of the mountain. It seemed as if an enormous giant had sculptured his own likeness on the precipice. Beneath the shadow of the mountain lived a small boy, Ernest. As a toddling child, he listened to his mother relate the strange prophecy passed down from generation to generation by the inhabitants of the valley that someday a great and wonderful man would come who would look like the visage on the mountain. In the years ahead Ernest never forgot the prophecy. At sunset he would gaze at the face and wonder who it would be. He became more and more interested in who it would be.

Finally the people felt sure they had found the person in a man of the valley who had become the richest man in the world. When he came home, they had prepared him a lovely home, but when they saw him, it wasn't he that had taken on the visage of the mountain. Years rolled swiftly on. Politicians, poets, and others passed by. Ernest became more and more interested in seeing the person.

In his advancing years he became more and more a man of wisdom. People looked to him for counsel and advice, and he was filled with humility and love for the valley and its people. He would gather in a little clearing near his home with the people for a time of prayer. One evening at sunset his face and head were outlined by the sky and sunset. The people recognized it was his face that had the image of the man on the mountain. And so we as Christians press on to be molded in the likeness of the Master, our great leader, savior and discipler. Do you bear the image of the Master?

3. WHAT JESUS DID WITH HIS DISCIPLES.[15]

Jesus' plan was to multiply workers. Jesus started it all, it then mov-

---

14. Ephesians 4:13.

15. Robert Coleman suggests these main themes in his book, *Master Plan of Evangelism*, (Old Tappan, New Jersey: Fleming H. Revell Company, 1976).

ed on to Peter, John, James and Paul. From Paul it went on to Timothy and his friends, and then on to others. By the fourth generation, such a project was really picking up steam. Jesus started with 12; if they were faithful, then it would turn to 144. In the fourth turn around there would be 1,728, and in the fifth, there would be 20,736 workers.

Can you see how important it is that we understand what Jesus did to bring about such a plentiful supply of workers in the Kingdom?

He chose men. These were men or women who were willing to serve. He chose John and Andrew.[16] Andrew then brought Peter and Philip, and they were chosen. He showed no haste, but was firm, careful and determined. He chose men who were willing to study and grow in the work to which they were called. They were not necessarily prominent men, but people who were willing to give themselves to the work of Jesus.

HE CHOSE A FEW

He centered on a few rather than trying to cover hundreds of people. He did not neglect the masses or His public ministry and preaching. He kept on with His disciples' daily training and working with them and preparing them for greater ministry and service. In a local church situation it is necessary to pick a few people, (three, four, five, maybe six people) from the body. These people can be called "Bold Ones." In the author's church, he began with ten. This was probably too many, but they were all volunteers. They prayed together, they studied the Bible together, they went out and sought the lost together. He selected those who were willing to grow, to learn, and to study. These became the core of the Bold Ones for Christ.

HE SPENT TIME WITH THEM

The second thing Jesus did with His disciples was to spend time with them. In examining the ministry of Jesus, you will find him eating, drinking and sleeping with them. It was not a formalized school with

---

16. John 1:35-40.

regular classes and a set time of meeting. It was in fact a marked contrast to the style of the scribes and Pharisees. But these men, by association, picked up his very life-style. They took trips together, retreats, boat rides, and had meals together. It must have been wonderful to have been with Jesus.

To implement discipleship within the body, the group must spend time together. Activities must include praying together, talking of needs, frustrations, and areas of growth or needed growth in their lives. A set time must be arranged and at this time the works of discipleship are implemented. If a preaching minister, be careful that you do not neglect the public ministry of the church, public teaching, public preaching, but never let discipleship be put on the back burner.

Here are some suggestions that will be helpful for you. Choose a Christian brother or two. Meet weekly with them, possibly for breakfast, or maybe even late in the evening. Talk of spiritual things, kingdom work. Talk of the problems and needs of the church. Pray for each other, love each other and go soul winning together. Have the wonderful experience of leading someone to Christ together.

HE DEMANDED COMMITMENT

A third thing that is necessary that we can learn from Jesus is that He demanded commitment from His disciples.[17] His teachings are literally filled with admonitions to commitment. Many didn't survive discipleship with Him and went back to their old life-style because obedience was expected. If they were unwilling to sacrifice and be obedient and were not willing to change their very style of living, Jesus would not accept them as disciples. They were expected to count the cost. Just a few stayed with Him. As they obeyed, they learned and grew. Obedience was the evidence of their love for Him.

When one enters the discipling plan in the author's church, he must make a commitment to finish what he has begun. He begins with ten weeks of lessons — lessons such as are contained in this book. Each week there is an hour of training in which he is expected to participate faithfully. After the hour of training, each spends an evening of calling

---

17. Matthew 11:39.

74

to share his faith with others. He is expected to disciple another person at the same time as he is being discipled. He is urged to make a lifetime commitment to this plan.

JESUS GAVE TO HIS DISCIPLES

He gave them His joy, His peace, His Holy Spirit. He shared His thoughts and insights with them. He taught them about deeper matters than the multitudes knew. His time with them was one long teaching session, parables, encounters with the Jews, times of teaching the lost, Nicodemus, the woman at the well, blind Bartemeus, and Zaccheus. They learned from His sermons and His public ministry as well as the private instruction.

The teaching of Jesus was most natural, very different from our classroom method today. His methods were the most varied possible. It was much as was hinted by Juan Carlos Ortiz when he was asked by a man who came to learn from him "when he was going to teach him anything?" Juan Carlos responded to this student, "if after two weeks you have learned nothing, you might as well go home. I can teach you nothing." Jesus' method was that they learned from His very life-style, from the way He lived and acted. Some classroom experience can be useful, on-the-job training is helpful, but in the end result, they had learned and received Christ by being with Him. He gave Himself to them. We must possess Christ ourselves, and when we do we can share him with another and another. As we grow, they grow, and the body of Christ grows.

In our church, part of the training process is for the disciples to learn from the one who is discipling them and adopt his life-style.

JESUS TAUGHT THEM BY HIS EXAMPLE[18]

They observed Jesus praying. The gospels refer to Jesus praying over twenty times. They learned about his prayer life. He taught them

---

18. John 13:15.

to pray.[19] He taught them by using scripture. The gospels show this emphatically. Especially as you look at the writings of the other Bible writers you will find that these disciples learned to use the Bible as Jesus had. He taught them to be soul winners. Everything Jesus did was related to His ministry of seeking and saving the lost.

Today in our churches, the disciple/discipler relationship should be one of prayer, Bible study and soul winning. The disciple adopts the lifestyle of the committed Christian discipler.

JESUS ASSIGNED DUTIES[20]

He sent out the twelve and He sent out the seventy after giving them instructions.[21] Jesus expected them to be obedient and do as he had told them. When they did not, they came back having failed in their mission.

Today in the church, we need to seek out those wanting instruction, wanting to grow in Christ, wanting to have a fruitful ministry. When Christians are unwilling to submit to the direction of the discipler they can gently be taught so that they will understand the need of cooperation as a disciple of Christ and what great benefits it can have in their lives. We should work with the promising prospects. They need to understand that it is a hard life. Sometimes it will bring division in the family, sometimes persecution. It may mean that many nights of family activities will have to be dropped in order to do the more important thing of reaching the world of Christ. Jesus teamed them up two by two.[22] Even after His resurrection He gave them His plan of conquest for the world.[23] He was assigning duties and giving them work to do.

Today a hard-working preacher trying to do everything that is needed in the church is a serious mistake. He may fall into the rut of mowing the lawn, cleaning the toilets, doing all of the calling on the sick, and the end result is that he becomes tired and disenchanted with the ministry. Burnout is the inevitable result. The wiser minister accepts the true com-

---

19. Matthew 6:9-13.
20. Matthew 4:19.
21. Luke 9:1-2, Matthew 10:1, Mark 6:7.
22. Mark 6:7.
23. Matthew 28:19.

mission God has given him of being an equipper and assigner of duties. He will learn to give jobs to people. He will help them to prepare to do these jobs. He will give them advice when it is needed, but then entrust them to go on with the work that they have been appointed to do. One of the very best ways to help people grow is to assign them duties. I am told that in the Mormon church there are over three thousand jobs that they assign members of their church to do. We could learn a lot from them in our churches today. We need to assign people jobs, keep them busy, help them to use the gifts God has given them. The Bible mentions over forty different gifts of the Spirit. If we can determine what people's gifts are and get everyone involved in using their gifts, it could break the clergy system within the church and bring the church back to fruitful ministry again.

CONTINUED SUPERVISION

Jesus continued to supervise those who were under His charge. Jesus received reports from the seventy and from the twelve as to how their work was going. After teaching, He discussed the deeper implications with them of what they had been taught and how this would apply to their ministries. On a number of occasions He adjusted their attitudes and views after they had been involved in ministry.

A new worker needs supervision. One should be assigned as discipler of the new person. They are partners for a season, or two seasons, or maybe even three seasons. They work together in teaching, praying, and the outreach program of the church. It is encouraging to meet back at the church after an evening of calling to share successes and failures while they are still fresh in their minds. This can also be a time of oversight and supervision.

Disciples need repeated instruction, suggestions, help and encouragement. This was Jesus' ministry to them.

REPRODUCTION WAS EXPECTED

Jesus called His disciples as fishers of men. He taught them that the gospel was like a grain of mustard seed. Jesus did not expect everyone to be saved. He did not expect that the work would be easy, but He did teach them and promise them that there would be precious fruit for their labors. Others would believe through their words.[24] The acid test of their discipleship was: did they carry on His ministry. The acid test of our discipling is: results, fruit, growth, carrying on the ministry to which we have been called. In the church, fruit can be expected and is a normal part of the plan. Spiritual growth will take place on the part of the individual disciple.

There have been about 100 people trained in discipleship within the author's church. These people are able to win souls. They help people walk the aisles to become Christians. They participate in baptizing, sometimes bring the people in without a paid minister present to help them. From this, the work is expanded and growth is the inevitable result in the Church. These kinds of results will take place if the church is careful in discipleship. The scriptural precedent is always best in the long run.

HOW DISCIPLESHIP WAS PRACTICED BY THE APOSTLES

Only four apostles left us writings. Depending on who wrote the book of Hebrews the count could possibly be five. Of these writers, Paul wrote the most, John next, then Matthew, Peter, James and Jude. Paul's writing matter is directed to churches and is the main source of information as to how discipleship worked out in actual practice among the apostles. The book of Acts gives us some insight from Luke's perspective.

The writings of Paul make it quite clear how important discipleship was to him and the success of his work. His writings are literally full of the names of fellow workers whom he had trained.

Here are some examples. In the sixteenth chapter of Romans Paul lists twenty-seven people who were his friends and fellow workers. There are both men and women. Phoebe, Prisca, Mary and Julia are women from the list, along with numerous others. It would probably not be accurate to say that all were people Paul had personally discipled, yet most were people Paul had recruited or helped develop in their

---

24. John 17:20.

ministries.

I Corinthians lists five people with whom Paul had labored and discipled. Colossians gives the names of ten fellow workers with Paul. Among these is Nympha, another lady worker. The point is, both men and women worked in discipleship. The women were very important to this work, as well as the men.

Timothy and Titus were men Paul helped train for ministry. By such methods his work was greatly expanded around the Mediterranean world. In Second Timothy Paul gives the name of nine more disciples. In the very short book of Titus there are five more disciples named.

All of these lists of disciples were not put into scripture by accident. They were included so we can learn from them. The ministry of Paul was more thoroughly recorded than the ministries of the other apostles. Yet, without a doubt, this same principle was applied by the rest of the apostles as the gospel spread around the whole known world (cf. Colossians 1:23).

We do not want to seem even the least bit critical of our many fine Bible colleges, but could it be true that we have left the work of discipleship to them and not carried it on in the local church? I fear this has too often been true.

There can be little doubt that discipleship was one great key to the success of the apostolic church of the first century. Paul alone mentions over fifty workers he discipled in only five of his writings. A complete listing would show many more.

In this author's church a great number of people have been trained for ministry by discipleship principles. This power can be put back to work in the church. Unfortunately, we have adopted another plan for our churches.

We live in the days of pragmatism, i.e. if it works, it's all right. Just because it works short term does not mean it is the answer to the need of the church in the long run. In the long run, the church has been hindered by some doing the work that the many should do. Just because a church is bursting with people does not mean it will change the course of the world. Shortcut methods have failed. The Bible plan begins more slowly, it takes more skill, it takes more determination, but people when they are committed to the program of discipleship and begin to take on the very nature of the master discipler can change the course of the world in which they live. In the author's church the Bible plan has worked well. At first there were ten, then there were twenty-five and then thirty. These people have then branched out on their own into ministries within the body. The church has been revitalized, the financial giving of the church has doubled, tripled and quadrupled. Discipleship has resulted in a steady stream of people coming to Christ. Some have given their lives to evangelism, preaching and new church evangelism. Every part of the church has been expanded and blessed because of the work of discipleship. No more important work could be entered into by a church than the work of discipleship. No other work has exceeded discipleship in renewing and blessing the church.

"Go into all the world and make disciples. . . . ."[25]

25. Matthew 28:19.

Chapter 5 Examination

1. Give a *full* definition of what the word "discipleship" means.

2. According to Matthew 28:19-20, how many people in the world are to be made disciples? Does this include all Christians?

3. What does the Hebrew word *talmid* mean?

4. Give five characteristics of a biblical disciple.

5. What can a proper understanding of this word do for the church today? List three things.

6. The end desired result of discipleship in our lives is what?

7. What seven things did Jesus do with his disciples?

8. How can discipleship be implemented in our local churches?

9. What three things are a must to discipleship in our churches today?

10. A wise minister will give time to training and discipleship. What must he be careful not to neglect while he is doing this?

6

GROWING CHURCHES OF TODAY

"And all who lived at Lydda and Sharon saw him, and they turn-ed to the Lord." Acts 9:35

It is not enough to be evangelical. We must be evangelistic. The evangelical church is a reservoir of pure water without a pipe running anywhere. If you will take the trouble to go to it and climb the embankment, you will get a good drink. The evangelistic church is a reservoir of pure water with a pipe to every heart in the community, and every nation in the world. Evangelical may mean truth on ice; evangelistic means truth on fire. Evangelical may be bombproof for defense; evangelistic means an army on the march with every face toward the enemy. Evangelical sings, "Hold the Fort, for I am coming;" evangelistic sings, "Storm the fort, for God is leading." The need of the church is not evangelicalism as a thing to fight for, but evangelism as a force to fight with. The evangelical creed merely held and defended becomes a fossil, only a thing of interest.

Several miles above Milton, Pa., when the ice was breaking up, a farmer got into one of his boats, purposing to pull it out of the river. A floating mass of ice struck it, breaking it loose from the bank, and carrying it and him out into the current. A neighbor, seeing the danger, mounted a horse and with all speed rode down to Milton. The people of the town gathered all the ropes they could secure, went out on the bridge, and suspended a line of dangling ropes from the bridge across the river. They could not tell at just what point the boat with the farmer would pass under, so they put a rope down every two or three feet clear across. By and by the farmer was seen, wet and cold standing in the boat half full of water, drifting down the rapid current. When he saw the ropes dangling within reach, he seized the nearest one, was drawn up and saved. Now, one rope might not have answered the purpose. The pastor hangs the rope of salvation from the pulpit, and the sinners present do not seem to get near it; but if the business men will hang out ropes, and you young men and women, mothers and wives, hang out ropes, sinners will certainly be saved.[1]

A CASE STUDY OF A QUALITY CHURCH

Words seem inadequate to describe the great task that needs to be done. The following example is given in the hope that such a growing, thriving, quality church might bring enlightenment to the reader. The church that is being used as an example will remain anonymous, but it is a real church in the Southern California area. This is a case study of an actual church, a quality church that seeks to minister with integrity.

First, let's talk about growth statistics in this particular church. In 1961, the average attendance in Sunday School was 132, with 181 attending church services. In 1975 for the first quarter, Sunday School attendance was eight hundred with 1,015 in worship services. The worship figures show this graph of growth: 1961, 181; 1970, 380 (during that year the church lost 118 people because of an aerospace layoff); 1971, 500. Late in 1971, a doctrinal problem caused the necessity of about eighty people being asked to leave the church. In 1972, the average attendance was 650; 1973, 780; 1974, 870; 1975, 1,015; 1984, 2,500; and 1987, 2,800. A person would probably ask first, "Do they have lovely spacious facilities?" The answer is, "No, the facilities are crowded; it is necessary for them to hold three church services as well as three Sunday Schools. People sat in movable chairs for several years and the church has classes everywhere."

The second area of growth in this church is that of personnel. The present preacher came in 1969 and had no paid help. In 1970, an assistant was hired to help with the many duties of the church. In 1973, a

---

1. William Evans, *Personal Soul Winning*, (Chicago: Moody Press, 1964), pp. 10-11.

man was hired to work full time in the area of music and calling; and later another man was hired to cover the areas of education and calling. In 1975, a second man was hired to work in the area of music and calling. The church now has a staff of seven full time ministers who work as equippers. In addition, there are several custodians and secretaries. The finances grew from less than $100,000 in 1967, to over $268,000 in 1975; the church was $12,000 ahead of their budget at the half way point of that year. Today their budget is nearly $1,000,000 annually. As has already been mentioned, the buildings are inadequate, and three services for Bible school and worship are necessary. The maximum number that can be seated in any one service is 850 persons.

What has been their strategy for growth and the factors which have brought it about? Has there been a large population increase? Strangely enough, the population has not grown in the area where the church is found.

What were the causes of church growth? Here are the reasons as listed by one of the preachers of that church. First, they said they created a vision of growth. The people had been discouraged, thinking that the church could not grow, that it had too many things hampering it and that there was no possible way that they could become a vital church. This attitude was changed. People were helped to see that it was God's will that the church grow, and after studying scripture they began to learn that the church not only could grow, but *must* grow if it was to be pleasing to Jesus Christ. The church began to set goals. They have used various means to obtain these goals, but always stress quality of teaching, of preaching, and of all that is done in the life of the church. People are not brought into the church through manipulation, but through careful teaching. They are discipled and made a part of the body.

Attention has been given to the church services. Special music is carefully done and only a person's best is good enough. No second-rate efforts for Jesus, please! Every week a review is made by the paid staff, of the church services and anything that was wrong is corrected for the following week. Every part of the church is undergirded by prayer and there is a strong trust in God and His working in their lives.[2]

---

2. Philippians 4:6 ". . . in everything by prayer and supplication with thanksgiving let your request be known to God."

The matter that is most strongly stressed by the leader of this dynamic church is that of evangelism. The evangelism of the church is centered in the concept that every Christian is to be prepared for ministry; thus, every Sunday School class has its own calling program that is constantly working. They specifically request that there be no phone calls, but that every call be a personal visit by teachers and class members, showing an interest in those who are either class members or potential class members.

There are four organized discipling programs within the church. The youth, juniors, and junior high call regularly and are trained from the time they are young people to be regular callers and to talk to the lost about Jesus Christ. The youth calling takes place one night a month.

The college group have a weekly discipling program on Monday night in which they go out in an organized way and talk to people about Christ. It is constantly stressed that every Christian is a minister all day long, all week long.

The adult calling program is led by a group called BOLD ONES FOR CHRIST.[3] In order to be involved in BOLD ONES the person must volunteer. No one is personally asked. They must take a specified number of nights of instruction and must call every Monday night. It is the goal of the church to have about twenty-five people involved in this BOLD ONES calling program. (The author's goal is 100 persons actively involved in discipling.)

Their fourth calling program is on a rotation basis, with the adult Sunday School classes canvassing new areas after mail-outs have been sent into the area for four weeks in advance. They have used three clever little cards, a different one mailed each week, to arouse interest on the part of the people receiving them. The fourth mail-out is a brochure explaining about the life of the church. They are then visited by a member of the church, given a packet of material concerning the church, and talked with about their relationship with Jesus Christ. All adult classes within the church have a calling program.

Every Monday night, one hundred survey type calls are made by people from the church. Much special calling is done by individuals and leaders within the church, including the paid staff as well as officers within the church, such as elders and deacons. Everyone is expected to

---

3. Ephesians 6:19. See Chapter 21 of this work.

call. The minister of music is expected to call on all the people involved in the choir. The minister of education is expected to call on all the people involved in the educational program within the church. One of the paid preachers is expected to call on all of the prospective members, and of course, all of the preachers share the responsibility of calling on those who are hospitalized. Much evangelistic calling is done.

The one most important ingredient in the life of this church, according to their preacher, is that every person is committed to the ministry. The whole church is geared to the concept of people being disciples for Jesus Christ.

THE TWENTY LARGEST SUNDAY SCHOOLS[4]

Certainly success breeds criticism. Humans have a tendency to want to criticize that which is successful, particularly if they themselves are not having the successes seen in others. The comments and observations made in this work do not come out of a spirit of negative criticism, but hopefully will be helpful when a church begins to grow. It is hoped the following observations might be warning flags. The criticism generally relates to a System II church.

First, we must face the problem of people manipulation. Because of man's nature, it is normal to want to be given gifts or to be made to feel important, but we must be careful not to make this the basic motivation for going to church. It would seem that that giving of gifts to get a person to attend church would be of a manipulative nature.

For example, one of the elders of a particular church showed up missing along with a carload of church members. When asked where he was, sheepishly he said, "I attended another church because they were giving away free records to everyone who came for the first time, and I wanted the record." His real motivation was not to learn about Jesus Christ but only to gratify a certain desire that he had. Many advocate such means. We do not question their motives, only their methods.

Another illustration is the giving away of motorcycles, Bibles, and everything from ice cream to color television sets to get people to come

---

4. I Thessalonians 5:21, "But examine everything carefully; hold fast to that which is good."

to church. Possibly this could be a legitimate means. A person might justify such experiences as the feeding of the five thousand by our Lord, as a means of His getting a crowd to hear Him preach. Strangely though, in the New Testament technique and methodology, this particular type of gimmick is not seen. Rather, the drawing power was Jesus Christ being upheld. How much stronger the tie would be if a genuinely concerned Christian took days and weeks to teach and disciple a person, helping them know Jesus and grow into His likeness. The goal is not a big attendance, but Christ-like people.

Another area of manipulation falls into a category that we might call "Madison Avenue" tactics. Certainly good technique is important in personal evangelism, but if our emphasis is on technique to the neglecting of Jesus Christ, Lord of Glory, then certainly we have questionable methodology. Such things as "ten easy steps to soul winning," tend to be gimmicky, rather than scriptural, practices.[5]

Also, we probably should mention teaching without integrity. This is teaching with a view to getting a response rather than teaching a person to really know Jesus Christ as Lord of the life. Much teaching has been done simply with a view of getting a decision and the decision isn't really legitimate. Such illegitimate teaching would include the lack of proper emphasis on repentance,[6] the lack of teaching one what faith really means,[7] or no commitment to Christian baptism.[8] Once, a man claimed to have won everyone on the airplane on which he was riding during a trip from Los Angeles to Chicago. Certainly such teaching did not have the type of integrity that we can imagine Jesus or Paul using.

After such methods were used in an Illinois church, there were sixty-four additions to the church. Great claim was made as to how great an evangelistic meeting they had had. However, of the sixty-four, only five ever returned to the church after the meeting, and these five were already steady church attenders.

The problem of manipulation is seen in whether the church's desire is simply to be big (to be just a bit bigger than another big church in

---

5. II Timothy 4:3 "For the time will come when they will not endure sound doctrine; but wanting to have their ears tickled, they will accumulate for themselves teachers in accordance to their own desires."

6. Luke 13:3.

7. Hebrews 11:6.

8. Acts 2:38; I Peter 3:21.

another area); or is the goal to be a good quality church that teaches Jesus Christ with integrity, even though the issues that must be dealt with are not always popular with the masses of people. We should remember the integrity of men like Isaiah, John the Baptist, Jesus, and Paul, who were unwilling to bend the message just for success in the sense of being big.

A church should continually question itself.[9] Is it really a New Testament Church? Does it continually test its methodology in the light of scripture? Does it continually examine the teaching technique in the light of scripture? Is the doctrine that is being taught founded in scripture? We must ask ourselves about mortality. How many of the people won really stay with the church after a few months? Is there a mortality rate of 60-90 precent of those who come and make confession and are baptized?[10] What sort of efforts are taken to conserve results? Many super-churches of today do make diligent efforts to conserve their results. What percentage of conservation actually takes place?

The question needs asking, "To what is the person won?" There is a simple rule of thumb that says that the type of effort by which a man is won will determine the type of Christian he will be. If a person is won to a church because of a flashy preacher, then he will be a flashy-preacher Christian and will be gone with the flashy preacher. If he is won by the gift of a motorcycle, then he will be a motorcycle Christian. If a person is won because of Jesus Christ, then the commitment should be lasting, a life-long commitment.[11]

When talking about the large Sunday Schools in America, we should take time to mention what is good. Generally the large Sunday Schools fall into the category of the System II church. The System II church is an improvement over the System I church. There is a lot we can learn from them; just because they are big does not make them bad. Usually a church grows because it is doing many things well. Yet, they

---

9. I Corinthians 3:10-15. Paul warns of the danger of building with "wood, hay, straw." The author's opinion is that we have a lot of "straw" building going on today. Let us be careful builders.

10. II Peter 2:21. "For it would be better for them not to have known the way of righteousness, than having known it, to turn away from the holy commandment delivered to them."

11. I Corinthians 2:2. "For I determined to know nothing among you except Jesus Christ and Him crucified."

too need evaluation in the light of the Biblical ideal. We can commend the growing churches because they are interested in growth and are interested in people knowing the message of Jesus Christ. Every church should be concerned about growth. We can commend these churches because of much personal evangelism being done by the members of the church. Certainly every church ought to have a dedication to personal evangelism. The church's commitment should be that of the New Testament, "And He gave some as apostles, and some as prophets, and some evangelists, and some as pastors and teachers for the equipping of the saints for the work of service to the building up of the body of Christ."[12] A mutual ministry of all members of the body of Christ will lead to growing churches.

---

12. Ephesians 4:11-12.

Chapter 6 Examination

1. A case study of a quality church is given in this chapter. List how it grew numerically.

2. Give a list of staff members of this church and when they were added.

3. List those things that helped this church to grow.

4. List the four discipleship programs in this church.

5. What is the one most important ingredient in the life of this great church?

6. What sort of negative things could be said about some of the twenty largest Sunday Schools in America?

7. What are some very positive things to be said for these large Sunday Schools?

8. A church being big is not bad, yet just because it is big does not mean it is scriptural. The rule is a church should be _____, then second, let it grow big.

7

MOTIVATION TO PERSONAL MINISTRY

"I can do all things through Him who strengthens me." Philippians 4:13

OVERCOMING FEAR

One of the things that the personal worker must deal with right from the beginning is fear. One personal evangelist of thirty-five years confessed that it still made him nervous to go and talk with people about Jesus Christ. Just how does a person cope with fear so he can go with real assurance? A very helpful principle is related in Corinthians. "Therefore, we are ambassadors for Christ, as though God were entreating through us; we beg you on behalf of Christ, be reconciled to God."[1]

Paul viewed himself as the very personal representative of Jesus and God. One must learn therefore, to go with dignity, realizing that he represents Jesus Christ. He has the backing of the universe's biggest company, and has the greatest product, the product of salvation for the

---

1. II Corinthians 5:20.

person's soul. Thus, the person should go to the door bravely, knock loudly, speak up, and be cheerful. Don't ever give the impression that what is offered is unimportant, because it is the most important product or gift ever presented to mankind.

As one grows in competence, nervousness will decrease. As a person learns what to say and the answers to questions (which are learned from raw experience) he will grow more confident.

When a person comes to a question for which he does not know the answer, learn to answer forthrightly, "I do not know, but I will see if I can find the answer." Everyone is ignorant, in different areas. It is no shame for a person to not know the answer to every question.

After a person has made several thousand calls, talking to people about Jesus Christ, he will more and more get used to the strain and begin to enjoy the challenge of representing Jesus Christ. Everyone has to cope with nerves. You are no different from the world's greatest callers. You will become more confident so you can talk to most any person without deep-seated fear.

OVERCOMING LAZINESS

Another motivational problem has to do with laziness. Most persons have the tendency to want to rest and relax, and take their ease in Zion, but it must be remembered that personal work is work. It will never be accomplished by the person who is lethargic. One must discipline himself much as the runner, swimmer, and musician would in doing that which is important to them. Overcoming laziness can be done by self-motivation, by setting goals, working towards those goals, and increasing the goals as one is reached, to move on to a higher goal.

It is important for the person who is afflicted with laziness to discipline himself to not let other "good" things take the place of personal evangelism. It is easy for one to get side-tracked in study, counseling, visiting with the familiar people and friends, or the sick, leaving the seeking of the lost until last. Discipline gets easier after a month of doing something. It has been said that a person acquires a habit after twenty-one days of doing a certain thing. Therefore, it is important that a person schedule his time so he can be effective in personal evangelism.

EARLY LACK OF SUCCESS

Often times early lack of success in calling can cause loss of enthusiasm. If a person will consistently make calls every week, it will only be a matter of time until he will have some successes which will build motivation to call. People do not call and do not have motivation to call because they often do not know how to call. They just don't know what to do or where to begin — thus, they develop the problem of fear and nerves and a loss of words when the occasion comes. The best means of overcoming this is competence, getting organized, and learning basic technique. After the basic technique has been learned, then a person can go into the work much more successfully.

When a dedicated Christian does not call, it certainly will build up a guilt complex that can plague his life, causing increasing apathy, discouragement, and the possibility of his eventually leaving the church. When a person, on the other hand, will be faithful in personal evangelism, it adds vitality to the life, so that the Christian continues to grow in knowledge and enthusiasm for the things of God. It has been said that an ounce of zeal is worth one hundred pounds of knowledge. Work is "foot pounds" moved and so one must be enthusiastic and get about the work of spreading the gospel of Jesus Christ. Success will come in time to the faithful caller.

THE GREATEST WORK IN THE WORLD

When the work of the gospel is put in its true light we begin to see how eternally important it is. Dr. Robert G. Lee quotes Dr. Charles L. Goodell as saying:

It is the great hour when a surgeon holds a scalpel at the end of which is life or death for the patient. It is a greater hour when a lawyer faces a jury, with the conviction that if he make a mistake, an innocent man will hang and a family be disgraced forever. But the greatest hour any human being ever faces is the hour when he stands before a man hastening to his condemnation and is commissioned to offer him a pardon that is to last for the eternities.[2]

---

2. Robert G. Lee, *How To Lead A Soul To Christ,* (Grand Rapids, Michigan: Zondervan Publishing House, 1955), p. 11. Used by permission.

Never will a person be involved in more important work than that of personal evangelism. It is time for the church to get its priorities clear. Can we get our eyes off the material things of this life and onto those things that are abiding and eternal? We surely can and we must. Being a caller is more important than building a skyscraper, bridge, or ship. It is eternal work.

Chapter 7 Examination

1. To overcome fear in personal evangelism, one should learn the lesson of II Cor. 5:20. What is that principle?

2. What should you do when someone asks you a question for which you do not know the answer?

3. How common is it for personal evangelists to be nervous?

4. What is a sure cure for laziness in personal evangelism?

5. What are sidetracks to personal evangelism we need to watch out for?

6. How do we overcome early lack of success in personal evangelism?

7. What is the most important work in the world?

8. Memorize Philippians 4:13 and write it from memory.

8

MORE ABOUT MOTIVATION

"Therefore, we are ambassadors for Christ, as though God were entreating through us . . . ." II Corinthians 5:20

A COMPULSION FROM ABOVE

The following things should help to motivate the Christian to do personal evangelism. First, he should recognize that there is a strong compulsion from above to do the work of personal evangelism. We have the command of Jesus Christ in Matthew 28:18-20. If we are to be His followers, we must heed His commands. Also, we have the invitation from above, given to the world by Jesus. "And let the one who is thirsty come; let the one who wishes take the water of life without cost."[1] So we have the command and invitation from above.

When a Christian begins to let Jesus be Lord of the life as Ephesians 1:22-23 suggests, then he will have a strong compulsion from the Holy Spirit of God to share his faith. A person ought to remember that Jesus was very angry with the man given talents who sat on them and did not

---

1. Revelation 22:17.

use them.[2] Certainly these facts should be a motivation from above for us to use the talents, the voice, that God has given us to share His message.

We, as Christians, are directed to go to every creature. In order to please our Lord we must have as a primary motive, compulsion from our Great Commander, Jesus Christ. If a Christian is willing to die for Christ, then let him determine to live for Him.

A COMPULSION FROM WITHIN

It is said that there is a compulsion from within. The filling of the Holy Spirit will motivate us as the apostle said, "For we cannot stop speaking what we have seen and heard."[3] Certainly there is a compulsion that comes from having the Holy Spirit within the life that will cause us to speak for Him. Christ living in us is a strong motivation for evangelism. "I have been crucified with Christ; and it is no longer I who live, but Christ lives in me; and the life which I now live in the flesh I live by faith in the Son of God, who loved me, and delivered Himself up for me."[4] So, with Christ in the life, a person will have a strong motivation or compulsion from within. When a person has shared the inner life with Christ and the Holy Spirit as the indwelling presence in his life, his concern will be deepened and the sharing of this concern will become a must. Sharing of this love and concern that Christ gives us will help us to do things that we could never do on our own, "For it is God who is at work in you, both to will and to work for His good pleasure."[5]

When a person has a real deep appreciation for what Jesus has done, he will want to share Jesus' wonderful grace with others. Love, wanting to share the good news of Jesus Christ, is the compulsion that comes from within the Christian.

A COMPULSION FROM AROUND

It is said that a strong compulsion comes from around us. Once a

---

2. Matthew 25:25-26.
3. Acts 4:20.
4. Galatians 2:20.
5. Philippians 2:13.

man said he regretted that he hadn't lived in the days of great unexplored frontiers. We do live in a day of great frontiers; frontiers of the mind, frontiers of the spirit, frontiers with the church, with a great expanding population calling from all around for us to share Jesus Christ. A troubled world calls us; the sin and moral decay of the fiber of society calls us; crisis in the home calls us. Even the psychiatrists today are having trouble. All of this is a strong call from around us saying, "Share Jesus Christ with us."

The godless materialism that is rampant, with its inability to satisfy, also tells us that people need something that will fill that spot in their heart shaped like a cross. As we see our nation becoming less Christian, it is a call from all around us. Much is said about social reform, yet the real need is for man to experience Christ in the heart to reform him from the inside out, not simply trying to reform him from the outside inwardly.

The need of men for the gospel should be a strong motivation to share Jesus Christ. Doctors are motivated, and teachers are motivated. What about Christians? The doctor cares for the body, but it will die and rot. He will always ultimately fail in his work. The teacher trains the mind and this, too, is temporary in the carnal man. The Christian worker trains the spiritual and eternal part, and educates the soul of man for eternity. It is imperative for the Christian worker to realize that the work he is doing is more valuable than building a bridge or a skyscraper, or a rocket to go to a foreign planet. The teacher of the souls of men is doing an eternal work.

As we think of the compulsion from around us, we must be aware that the responsibility for the salvation of all men is placed upon us. Could we map a strategy to get it done? Could we think big enough and plan in such a way that this great world-wide task could be accomplished in our lifetime? Could we, with the modern means of television, radio, printing, and travel accomplish the same kind of results that were accomplished by the early church? Certainly we can, and we must in our day.

As an additional motivation from around us, there is the cry of human need. There are so many suffering, despondent, and despairing people whose lives are wrecked. What they really need is to see the purpose and meaning of life. They need to be placed in contact with the power of God to begin living in harmony with all of creation through

Jesus Christ. The cry of human need is so evident to us today we *must* do something. The cry from around us should be heeded. God almost never gives the gospel without using some human instrumentality. That human instrumentality is you or me. We must be aware of the great compulsion from around us.

BE HAPPY

Another motivation for personal evangelism is the desire to be happy. Much unhappiness is bound up in guilt — guilt about not living up to the commands of Jesus, or about not living the full Christian life as a person ought. Nothing will add deeper or richer happiness to a person's life than that of bringing souls to Jesus Christ. There is no better way to become happy than by helping people and investing your life in others. There is no better way to help people than to place them in contact with Jesus, the Savior. It is a very strong motivation to be happy and useful to mankind, to bring about a purging of society, and to bring happiness in the home and in the interpersonal relationship. The joy of bringing a person to salvation is one of the greatest of all Christian experiences. Satan robs us when he gets us to neglect this supremely important task.

SEEING THE LOST IN THEIR TRUE LIGHT

Finally, a great motivation for personal evangelism is getting a proper perspective of the lost. When we see the lost in their true light and realize how condemned, how undone, and how hopeless their present and future existence is, then we will begin to snatch souls from the fire and begin to work diligently, feverishly in the all-consuming work of personal evangelism. Get a proper perspective of lost people and it will be a great motivation for success in personal evangelism. Get a picture of the awfulness of Hell. Remember the rich man.[6] Smell the seared flesh of Hell and then picture your loved ones there.

Dr. Robert Schuller was called by someone who lived in the red light

------

6. Luke 16:19.

district of Los Angeles to talk to a dying prostitute. She had terminal venereal disease. He took one of his elders along with him to protect his character. He talked with her of her soul's salvation. As he left her, he remembered that the niece of the elder was not saved. Dr. Schuller said, "Your niece plays the organ for the church. She is clean and a nice girl, fifteen years old. She has never been out in sin much. You are not bothered about her much, but are real upset by the condition of this lady. But your niece is as unconverted and is going to Hell with these harlots and drunkards and with every other lewd and wicked man and woman in the world who turns down Christ." For a moment Dr. Schuller said he thought he would be hit. But the next Sunday, the young niece came to accept Christ. The uncle saw her in her true light.

Many more invitations could be added to this list. Let the love of God shine through you.

Chapter 8 Examination

1. List the five motivational factors of chapter eight.

2. Briefly, explain each of these motivations.

3. Doctors care for the _____, teachers care for the
_____, seasonal evangelists care for the
_____.

4. What is the blessed result in the life of the soul winner that comes as a by-product of leading souls to Christ?

5. Explain the condition of lost people. How does this help motivate you?

9

GETTING ORGANIZED — ESPECIALLY FOR PREACHERS

"And everyone who competes in the games exercises self-control in all things. They do it to receive a perishable wreath, but we an imperishable. Therefore I run in such a way, as not without aim: I box in such a way, as not beating the air, but I buffet my body and make it my slave . . . ." I Corinthians 9:25-27

Unless a person is willing to place a high priority on personal evangelism, it probably will not get done.[1] If the preacher places a higher priority on study, organization, counseling, or other aspects of the life or work of the church, it will be easy for these things to take precedence over personal evangelism. The result is that the church does not grow, and in a short time, problems of all sorts begin to creep into the church. The smell of death is upon the church. If a person will place a high priority on personal evangelism, he will make the opportunity to be with people. As he begins to call, he will begin to be in touch with what is going on in the church. He will acquire a new feeling for what is happening; he'll understand people's problems. Preaching will take on a new meaning, and even study will have new significance, as the leader, preacher, understands what is going on in the church. The preacher will develop a sixth sense about the needs of his people. Per-

---

1. Acts 20:26-27; I Corinthians 9:19-23; These passages illustrate the high priority the apostle placed on his soul winning activities.

105

sonal evangelism can be a tonic, like a dose of vitamins for the church and preacher, bringing real vitality to them both.

Unless the preacher places a high priority on personal evangelism, it is likely the elders won't, the deacons won't, the Sunday School teachers won't, the choir leader and choir members won't, and so it spreads throughout the whole church. When the preacher begins to place a high priority on evangelism, it will be necessary for him to get organized.

MAKING A SCHEDULE

Dr. Jack Hyles offers the following schedule as a suggested means of organizing a preacher's work week.[2]

He suggests that on Monday, the preacher sleep late and get home early. It should be a light day, with office hours perhaps from 9:00-4:00, taking care of business, counseling, shut-ins and hospital visits; this will help the minister rest from Sunday. Monday is a good day to go home early and take the family out to eat in the evening.

Tuesday mornings are a good time for business, counseling, and letters. Tuesday afternoon can be spent with the children.

Wednesday morning is for business, counseling, letters, etc. Wednesday afternoon is for study.

On Thursday morning, plan church visitation for Thursday evening, and take care of other miscellaneous duties as time permits. Thursday afternoon is for soul-winning and visitation.

On Friday morning, plan for the services on Sunday with study and other miscellaneous tasks. Spend Friday afternoons on soul-winning and visitation.

Saturday morning do work around the house, such as mowing the yard or repairing items until about 11:00 A.M. A good time for prospect visitation is between eleven o'clock and one o'clock on Saturday. Babysit for the wife on Saturday afternoon while she goes to the store and has some time alone. Spend Saturday night in prayer, preparation, and meditation of the heart for Sunday. Bear in mind that the preparation of the mind should have already been made. Spending some time

---

2. Dr. Jack Hyles, *Let's Build An Evangelistic Church*, (Murfreesboro, Tennessee: Sword of the Lord Publishers, 1962), pp. 121-122.

preparing the heart for Sunday is very important.

Sunday is the day for public services, of course, with rest, study, and meditation in the afternoon. You'll notice in this schedule that Dr. Hyles has included quite a bit of time for personal evangelism. Even though he is the preacher of a church with thousands in attendance on Sunday, he still takes time for personal evangelism. It is very important for us to realize that we can organize our work week so that we can call.

Another author suggests:

> If no other time can be given, set aside the hours from half-past six to nine o'clock one evening per week. Many churches include a definite calling night in their schedules. In any case, choose a definite time and hold it sacred to the purpose. Incidentally, one of the greatest values of visiting by appointment is the discipline it affords the caller. A team of ladies calling on ladies may find the afternoon preferable. Use judgment, considering the interest and convenience of those called upon quite as much as you do your own interest and convenience.[3]

A schedule that the author has used with good success is the following:

Monday is to be used as a day of rest and relaxation. People are tired from the weekend and usually it is a very poor time to call. They will be wanting to lie around the house after work and rest from the activities of the weekend. It is a good time to sleep late and do odd jobs, rest, shop, play golf, go to bed early.

Tuesday morning: go to the office at a regular set time, say nine o'clock; you'll work late several evenings a week so remember that it is not awfully important to be at the office at the crack of dawn unless you desire to do so. Write letters, be businesslike, neat and proper. Take care of church administration, make appointments for counseling, plan, take care of personal devotions, read, and study. In the afternoons give time to calling. Go to the hospital or nursing homes first thing in the afternoon. Visit guests who were at the church on the past Sunday, making every effort to visit them early in the week. They will know that you really care about them if you do so. It is probably advisable that a person quit calling by 4:30 P.M., as this gets into the dinner hour.

---

3. Joe Ellis, *The Personal Evangelist,* (Cincinnati, Ohio: Standard Publishing, 1964), p. 74.

Wives will be preparing dinner for their husbands and families, and will resent being interrupted. Then from seven o'clock to nine o'clock, call on the best prospects that you have on your prospect list. Make these decision calls. Plan that Tuesday night will be given to those who are most likely to respond to the gospel invitation on the following Sunday. Normally, Tuesday night is a very good night to call, because it is sort of in the middle of the week. Later in the week, people will be getting ready for the weekend, taking care of activities at school, work, or church functions, and it is the author's opinion that Tuesday night is usually one of the best nights to call.

On Wednesday: go to the office at nine o'clock, get your sermon plans well begun and organized. Take time for personal devotion and prayer. Prepare your prayer meeting lessons or other lessons that must be given during the course of the week. Get the church paper out of the way and finalized and in the mail. Call during the afternoon on prospects or members needing visitation. Seek to find the best prospects so you can call on both husband and wife in the evening. If you do not have anyone to call on, check the chapter on developing prospects. Wednesday evening is often involved in church services.

Thursday: again be at the office at nine o'clock. Have Sunday morning's sermon finished and well in hand; have it ready to preach. Pray about it Thursday, Friday, and Saturday; let it cook and jell in the mind and become thoroughly familiar with it. If a person does this well, it could easily take the whole morning. You may have to block this space on your calendar to keep from being interrupted. After lunch, make hospital calls, visit the sick and the shut-ins. Hospital visitation should be about three times a week. Some emergencies will arise, making more visits necessary at times. Again, begin to visit prospective members and members who may be backslidden or not showing proper interest. Spend the afternoon in visitation and being among the people. This will help you to understand the people's needs. It will give relevance to your preaching. Quit at 4:30 in the evening, go home and spend a little time with your wife and family. From seven o'clock to nine o'clock, again visit your best prospects and press for decisions. This is also a fairly good night to call.

Friday: at nine o'clock, finish the Sunday evening sermon. Have it completely finished and ready to preach. Do some counseling, pray and take care of other duties that arose in the course of the week. From twelve o'clock until after lunch, call and run errands for the church. It is the author's opinion this is the poorest afternoon of the week to call. From 3:30 P.M. on, when the children are out of school, spend time with the family, take your wife to town, and make this a family night. Reserve it for some special type of activity for the children or your wife.

Saturday morning, a preacher might want to be at the office again at nine o'clock to finish up last minute office work. Be sure Sunday School lessons are well in line and the Sunday evening sermon is clearly in mind. Pray about your sermons. At noon, or from eleven o'clock until about one o'clock, a person can make several last minute calls on prospective members. Quit early in the afternoon and spend the afternoon relaxing and getting ready for Sunday. Saturday afternoon is a good time to spend with the family.

Sunday: the preacher will want to be at the office early enough to go over his sermons and pray again. Few calls should be made on Sunday except for emergency calls. Sunday afternoon is probably one of the poorest days of the week to call. Seldom does an absentee member wish for the minister to show up on Sunday afternoon to catch him relaxing around the house, not nearly as sick as he had hoped the preacher would think he would be. Those who were in church do not need a call. Let the elders and deacons of the church take communion to those who are sick or shut-in and need visitation from the church.

OVERCOMING OBSTACLES

Anytime a person is involved in useful work for the kingdom of Christ, the devil will make one hundred interruptions to keep him from doing it.[4] These interruptions will take the form of good things: study, counseling, funerals, weddings, and even sickness. If a person will, week after week, press on with the schedule he has made, he will find that the schedule will begin to work and the obstacles will seem to fade out of the way. However, never get too busy to spend the necessary time with the people of the church.

Be careful not to get into the habit of visiting friends and those peo-

---

4. I Thessalonians 2:18 "For we wanted to come to you — I, Paul, more than once — and yet Satan thwarted (i.e. hindered) us."

ple on whom you find it easy to call. To see what type of people you have been calling on, check your schedule. Keep a list every week of those you have visited. A good suggestion is to keep a little pocket calendar book to list the names of people called upon. This will become a permanent record.

Be careful that you do not get into the habit of playing golf two or three afternoons a week with some prospective member. It is not wrong to play golf, but a person can get into the habit of doing something that will rob him of the time he needs to be effective. Work around interruptions, instead of letting interruptions take the place of personal evangelism. Be very careful that you do not get bogged down in calling on people who are poor prospects and who show little interest in the work of the church.

FINDING THE BEST TIMES TO CALL

What are the best times to call? Each community will have its own characteristics. Farm people, for example, characteristically get up early and go to bed early. The night of some big doings in town, whether it be a ball game or other social activity, might be a poor time to call. Different seasons of the year will change the time when it is best to call. It is usually a good time to call when it is bitterly cold or snowy outside. People will be at home. If the caller is perceptive he will find the times of the week when it is generally best to do visitation in his community. When a person has determined what time is best, work that time into the schedule and use your time wisely.

KEEP TRACK OF PROSPECTS

It is important to keep track of prospects. How should this be done? Three-by-five file cards can be purchased very reasonably. These cards can have the name of the prospect typed on one side with the name, address, phone number, and basic facts about the person on the other. There will still be room on the card to make other notations. This stack of file cards can be rather like a person's garden. Some prospects will be good prospects and some will not be quite so good. Some will even be poor prospects. They can be kept, worked, and cultivated. Stop by and visit with people from time to time even though they are poor prospects. There will usually be someone in the stack of cards who is near a decision. This stack of cards can be kept in the automobile that you drive, with a rubber band around them. Use this as a master file. The preacher can give copies of these cards to other people for calling. As the week progresses sort through the cards to find people who are about ready for a decision. Sort out the ones to be called on this week and put them on the top of the pile. Plan evening calls on those who are best prospects. If possible, make appointments with those to be called upon on Tuesday and Thursday evenings. Always keep a master file for the church of those who are your prospects. In working with these prospects, work those who are most interested first. Do very much as you would with your garden. Cultivate and pick the ripe fruit.

VISITATION OF WOMEN

Men can have a successful ministry to women. We can learn this from the ministry of Jesus, himself. Jesus had a great influence in the lives of many women, both married and single, both upright and sinful. John 4:7-33 gives the account of the woman of Samaria. She had been married five times and was then living with a man who was not her husband. We can learn some things from Jesus' practice. He met and talked with her in a public place. It was where other people came and went. He did not see her in a private place. His disciples were observers of the scene.

On other occasions Jesus taught and ministered to women. The woman taken in the act of adultery is another example, John 8:1-11. We could recall to our minds the time when Mary anointed Jesus' feet with ointment and dried His feet with her hair, John 11:2 and 12:1-3. This latter occasion did bring criticism of Jesus from Judas. Here again Jesus' contact with women was in a public place and left Him beyond the realm of credible criticism. Women have been the downfall of many men of God.

A word should be said about calling on women alone. Many preachers will use the problem of calling on women alone as an excuse for not calling at all. They will make the excuse that they are afraid to go to the house during the day when the husband is not home. The result is, they do not call at all. Normally it is safe to call on ladies in the home, *during the day*. The children will be around and if a person is careful to make brief calls, no one will be suspicious unless one begins to call on the same house day after day, or week after week. A person should be careful to develop a sixth sense about a woman who might have a strange attraction for the preacher. When such is observed, stay away from this home at all costs. Normally, it is unnecessary to have someone along while calling. If a person feels the least bit uneasy, get out and get out immediately. Spot trouble early, see that there may be trouble coming and move away; dismiss yourself cordially and do not go back to that place alone. These trouble spots will be few if a person maintains the type of integrity that should be found on the part of a man of God. If you feel uneasy and yet know that you should make a call, take your wife or an elder along. People have a high respect for a minister of God and if a person uses good common sense there will be little talk about his activities as long as he is really maintaining Christian principles and behavior.

Chapter 9 Examination

1. What is necessary if we are to find time for personal evangelism?

2. What is the inevitable result of lack of evangelism in a church?

3. Make a week's schedule showing your whole week's activities. Show the time you will use for personal evangelism. Show a knowledge of the schedules in the text.

4. List several obstacles that will arise to prevent your calling. How will you overcome these?

5. How should you keep a record of your calls?

6. How can you find the best time to call?

7. Prepare a prospect list of twenty or more prospects upon whom you are calling.

8. What is a wise plan in calling on women?

10

COMMON SENSE HOW-TO

". . . be shrewd as serpents, and innocent as doves." Matthew 10:16

The process of getting into the house can be a problem to a person who is inexperienced in calling. It is quite a simple process to get into the house. A person needs to approach the door, knock loudly, stand in plain view, and as soon as the person comes to the door, explain his mission. You can say, "My name is Fred Smith. I'm from First Christian Church and I'm here to talk to you about Christ." Don't be timid.

The author's early experiences were varied and many of them were not as positive as they could have been because of being timid. After a little while it became apparent that most people are happy to have a church worker come on behalf of Christ. People will show kindness to the caller if he is careful to be thoughtful, to be kind, and to watch the person who is being called upon. Watchfulness will indicate right away if you have come at a bad time. If the lady is washing her hair, obviously it is not a good time to stay for a call. When a person answers the door, be sensitive to the situation within. Watch the person's actions carefully. If they are still eating, if there is sickness, if they have company, or if they have their coats on and are ready to leave, excuse yourself graciously, say that you were in the neighborhood and will be happy to call back at a later time. Remember, when you come unannounced, you should be careful of their feelings; they did not know that you were coming and may have had other important plans for themselves and their family.

It is quite normal to find no one at home when calling. This is an excellent time to leave a calling card. The calling card left at the house should not be a tract with lots of teaching upon it, simply a professionally done card stating the name of the church and the name of the caller. It should be printed to look like a business card that one would expect to receive from a lawyer or professional person in the community. The card should say only a very few things.

When no one is home, always leave a card on the door in a spot that is easily seen. The card will communicate your concern. All that has been said is that you cared enough to come in person to their house to talk to them about the Lord. If the person had been home, you might have put your foot in your mouth by something that you had said. But a card left on the door is a very positive way of saying "I care about you; I care about your soul and your spiritual needs." Often when a person is not home, just the card will communicate enough concern to bring that person to church the following Sunday. Use calling cards profusely.

Do you need an appointment to call? Many times it is wise to make an appointment in advance. Try to analyze the people. Professional people, doctors, and lawyers, are usually very busy. It is important for you to have an appointment before calling on them; but with the average call, that usually is not necessary. If a person is very careful not to intrude when someone is obviously busy, he will encounter very few problems. As a general rule, a preacher can call in the afternoons by just dropping by and no one will really mind. An important evening call can best be made if an appointment is made in advance.

It is well to determine what type of call you are going to make before going to the house. Many different authors have written about the types of calls. Generally they are divided into four classifications. It is impossible to categorize all calls, because no two calls are exactly alike, but generally the following information will be helpful.

FOUR TYPES OF CALLS

Initial calls are generally friendly calls. If a person does not consider you as his friend, it is nearly impossible to lead that person to Christ. It is unwise to walk up to a total stranger, grab him by the collar and blurt out, "Friend, are you saved?" They deserve better, and other methods will bring more lasting results. Although it is true that we should take every opportunity to continually talk to persons about Christ — whether it be in the grocery store, gas station, or on the airplane — it is wise to make a friend out of them in the process of teaching them about Christ. This can be a time of fellowship, of getting acquainted, a time of listening and getting to know the person and his family. It is a time of being friendly and showing genuine concern. The better you know and understand the person, the better you can help him. It is always good during the friendly call to talk about things of interest to them such as their house, kids, family, vocation, hobbies, and the yard. Whatever is of importance to them can generally be learned by looking around the house. Do not talk about yourself or others endlessly. Become their friend.

During this time, the three-by-five file cards previously mentioned can be of great help. After the caller has left the house and driven a block or two away, he can stop and make a few notes of the important facts about the family, the people's names, their interest, and their background.

The friendly call is very important to personal evangelism. Much time should be spent in making friendly calls on people. People will be caught a little off guard if the preacher comes and does not begin immediately to preach to them. They will respond later by saying, "I like this man. He is concerned about me as a person as well as concerned about the growth of the church and about my spiritual needs."

Usually people will not be willing to talk about deep spiritual or personal needs until they become confident that the person is concerned about them and loves them deeply. So often, real good calling can only take place after a friendship or trust has been established. Do not use this as an excuse for not talking to everyone you meet day by day, but just keep this in the back of your mind. If you want to be a real help to a person, show yourself to be a genuine friend.

The second type of call is the church-related call. Your friendly call should awaken an interest in the church. As you drive to the home, review the information on the prospect card. When you arrive at the house, visit with the person in a friendly manner for a few minutes, then make the necessary transition. You could say, "I am here on behalf of First Christian Church." If the person asks questions about the church, this is a prime opportunity to move on to a type two call. Invite them to the church meetings and explain about the church. Give an accurate and enthusiastic description of the church. Be careful to stress the positive. It is not necessary to air any dirty linen, but give a careful, accurate, honest description of the good things that can be said about the church. Be sure that they know where and when the services take place and how they can be involved in these services. Tell of the friendly nature of the church, and be sure that it is true.

If at all possible, arrange to pick them up on their first visit to the church. Sit with them, introduce them to their Sunday School class, and make them feel welcome. As you visit with them in the church-related call, be sure to listen for further information about their background or feelings.

You will probably have an opportunity to answer questions that will arise in their minds about the church. Again, make careful notes after the call. Give them a folder telling about the church if such is available. If not, make one up.

Be confident, friendly, and warm with people. Remember that you are there on behalf of the Lord Jesus Christ. You are an ambassador for Christ and the job that you are doing is one of the most important things that can happen in the life of the family.

The next type of call is the teaching call. Appointments should be made, when possible, for teaching calls. When making a church-related call, a person could ask if the family would like someone to come to their home and teach them. The nature of the teaching call will depend upon the background of the person.[1] The callers should have a clear idea of what they are going to do during the call, before they go into the house. The strategy should be planned in advance if possible. This is so time won't be wasted and the conversation just meander from here to there. Several different types of teaching calls are possible. Some possibilities are: (1) out of town member of a New Testament Church, already a Christian; (2) a denominational person from a different background who needs to know about the New Testament church; or

---

1. Suggestions as to how one should teach people with different kinds of background is given in Chapters 11-14.

(3) a person coming from a Catholic, Mormon, or Jehovah Witness background. But the real questions that the person probably will need dealt with will be very basic. The teaching plan that is suggested in Chapter 11 will be useful in most cases.

Always remember that a planned presentation is a must if a person is to be brought to a decision for Christ with integrity. As you will notice in Chapter 11, the Bible chain reference is an easy, good means of teaching, especially for a person who is not too familiar with the Bible. Flip charts have their place. Many have been prepared and are available through Christian bookstores. Filmstrips are available from several sources and can be used to good advantage.

Remember, in the teaching call, be friendly and get to the point. Usually a teaching call need not last more than one hour, so don't stay too long. Be sensitive to their feelings. Learn to observe the person carefully to determine what he is feeling. Learn to show the love of Christ by your life.

The fourth type of call is the decision call. Any of the previous calls may become a decision call at any time. Be ready. Obviously a teaching call may and should end in a decision. There comes a time when we must go seeking action. When a person has been called on several times and has done nothing about church membership, has not come to repentance, made a public confession or been baptized, nor returned to steadfastness, then do not be afraid to ask questions. Ask questions that you know will elicit a positive answer, i.e., "You do believe in Jesus Christ, don't you?" or, "You do try to turn from sin and live a good life, don't you?" or, "Would you like to be baptized into Christ?" or, "You have been thinking about becoming a member of the local fellowship, haven't you?"

Remember that when you are there for a decision call, the object is to get a decision with integrity. It is not a time of arm twisting, manipulation, or putting the person into a corner until they are embarrassed and make a decision out of fear. It is a time of kindly, carefully, patiently leading the person to deal with his needs, not the needs of the caller. If a person will come with a deep motivation of love, he will not be guilty of bringing people to phony decisions.

Now, let's turn our attention back to what happens at the door. Let me remind you that when you arrive at the house, it is always wise for you to state your purpose, that is, "I am here to visit with you a little

119

while about the church." This would be a good approach for the friendly call. Or if you are there on a church-related call, "I am here on behalf of the church and I would like to talk to you a little while about various things that are offered to you by our church." Or, if you are there on a teaching mission, you could tell the people, "I'm here to study the Bible with you tonight." Or, as you enter the house, you might say, "I am here tonight because we've studied the Bible and we're hoping to help you with a decision about the matter of your church membership or becoming a Christian." It helps as you enter the house for your purpose to be clearly known. Whether it be a type two or four call, always let the people know that you are there on behalf of the church. Set their minds at ease in the first five minutes of your visit as to the exact reason for your being there.

When you enter the house, begin your call by being conversational and friendly. Remember that you have entered another person's home. It is his castle and it is not a place for you to argue, intimidate, or condemn. Be magnanimous and kind and you will be a good representative for Jesus Christ.

As you begin to make one of these four types of calls, it is a must to keep in mind the seven steps of a good interview.[2]

1. BEFORE YOU REACH THE DOOR

All calling should begin with prayer. This prayer can be silently offered as you drive to the home, or audibly spoken with a partner who is calling with you. It is important to pray that the Holy Spirit go before you and that you will be given the confidence that comes from God, not man. As you go to the house, it is always well to review the known facts about the people. Know the prospect's name well. If you know about his job, children, and other information, it will help you. Plan the strategy and decide before you get to the door what you are going to do, what the purpose of the evening's call will be. Keep your eyes and ears open for signs of the person's inner feeling. The person may be a big, strong logger, appearing rough and tough, but often these strong-

---

2. Joe Ellis, *The Personal Evangelist*, (Cincinnati, Ohio: Standard Publishing, 1964), pp. 83-92.

appearing people will become quite nervous when someone from the church calls. Do not think that they are uneasy with you, necessarily, but they are made uneasy because they realize their relationship is not right with Jesus Christ. A call from the church is somewhat threatening to them and shortness will not mean that they do not like you, are afraid of you, or wish that you hadn't come; only that they realize you are a representative of God, and the Holy Spirit has already begun to work in their lives.

Note the condition of the lawn, the house, the car. These are good clues as to the type of people you will find inside the house.

2. AT THE DOOR.

The first few minutes of a call are very important. Either you will make a good impression or a bad one. Knock firmly. A knock has a personality. It does not need to be such a loud knock that it breaks down the door; neither does it need to be such a timid little peck that a person cannot hear. Knock firmly and knock several times right to begin with, so that a person in the house can hear. Ring the doorbell a couple of times, but do not punch it six or eight times. If you listen carefully you can hear if it has rung.

Then step back in plain view so that the person does not need to hunt for you behind the door as it opens. Smile when he comes to the door and ask the person's name. You can say, "Are you Mr. Jones?" If the person says, "Yes, I am Mr. Jones," then introduce yourself and say that you are from the church and ask if you might step into the house. Few people will be rude enough to leave you standing on the porch. If they reject you or say, "I do not wish to have you come into the house," then excuse yourself and be on your way. When you have entered the house, greet all who are present, warmly and genuinely.

3. THE OPENING.

An opening may be offensive, awkward, or charming. Different people demand a different approach. Paul said that he became all things to all men that he might win some. Do not try to impress the person with your large store of jokes, your cunningness, or your intellect. Just be yourself, be friendly, be warm and kind. Be aware of sickness or other things that might be happening in the home. If the home is in a shamble (some homes are always in shambles) and obviously it is a bad time to call, then excuse yourself and come back at a later date. Visit warmly with the person, remembering that a good call does not have to be lengthy; in fact, good calls are seldom lengthy calls. A person does not need to stay an hour and a half or two hours to make a good call.

4. THE TRANSITION.

It is a critical time when a person seeks to shift the call to the main purpose at hand, whether it be a type one or type four call. Most people have trouble with transitions. The main problem is that of fear. Do not be afraid to make the transition. Shift to the main purpose of the call with grace and ease.

Let's use a decision call as an example. After you have visited for a few moments, you could say, "John, most of us are Christians because someone helped us to decide. Your interest in the church and Christ is most gratifying and we would like to talk with you about making the all-important step to become a Christian. I am a Christian today because someone helped me make this decision. I appreciated their concern and love so deeply that I have come this evening to help you with that important step to become a Christian."

The discussion is now open and it has been opened warmly, carefully, and the conversation can go on about the issues. The person may say, "I have a number of questions that I would like to ask." So you can deal with the questions, one by one. They may have questions about the nature of baptism or they may have questions about a doctrinal issue in the church or even may have some objections. If the person has objections, this is simply saying, "I'm still not convinced." This does not mean that you should give up at that point, but that you should deal with the objections one by one, lovingly, kindly, and carefully, considering each one as being really significant.

5. THE DISCUSSION.

Whether it be a type one or any of the other three types of calls, turn tactfully to the business at hand. It may be that this is a teaching call. If it is, then you can go right on to teaching them the Roman road, or some other type of planned presentation. But get to the business at hand and have the discussion for which you have come. As soon as the discussion has been brought to a careful conclusion (hopefully the discussion has not taken more than about thirty minutes at the most) a person should move on the climax.

6. THE CLIMAX.

Most calls will move right into the climax without a person having to work towards it. When the presentation has been made and the person has said, "Yes, I would like to become a Christian," and you know he wants to accept Christ, then arrangements should be made for him to make his public confession and be baptized into Christ.

7. THE CLOSING.

The closing need only last a very few moments: each call must be concluded. It is best to close with a few well chosen words, thanking them for their hospitality. If it is a teaching or decision call, it is important that the call be concluded with prayer. As soon as the prayer has been said, a natural break has been made and a person can leave with a broad smile and a warm handshake. When a person is making one of these four types of calls, remember that it can change from a type one to a type two, three, or four call easily.

WHAT TO DO WITH HARD QUESTIONS.

What does a person do with hard questions? One of the things that make callers nervous is the thought that they may be asked a question for which they do not have an answer. This is possible no matter how capable and qualified the caller may be. It is always easier to ask questions than to answer them. A person should remember the words, "I don't know," and use them whenever a question is asked for which they do not have the answer. The caller's integrity will be enhanced in the eyes of the person who is being called on and he will appreciate your honesty. You will be more relaxed realizing you do not always have to have an answer. Next, after saying, "I don't know," tell the person, "but I will find out. I will check my resources."

When you give an answer and say, "I know this is true," be certain that you know it is true. Be sure of the facts before you say that you know. Be careful in answering a person's questions. Be sure a Biblical answer is given. If the scriptures speak on the subject, let the scriptures speak, and leave it with what the scripture says.

Use resources. For the caller in the church, a good resource may be the preacher, or a knowledgeable elder. Such sources as *International Standard Bible Encyclopedia* or commentaries can be used. A person can turn to the church library as a good source. Resource material is available so that one can give answers to hard questions.

It is always well to remember that there are some questions with which theologians have wrestled almost since the beginning of the church. There are some questions that you will not be able to answer. Most of the basic questions that arise in a call we can answer and be sure about, as the scriptures speak plainly on most issues. If they do, you are on safe ground.

Remember the four types of calls: friendly, church-related, teaching, and decision. All calls will not fit into these categories. These will give you a basic handle to help you in planning your calls.

The seven steps of an interview may not always be apparent, but generally will be present. Analyze your calling to see if you are fitting everything in that should be there.

Remember, questions and objections are the caller's encouragement to teach the person the truth. Don't give up. Objections should be like saying "sic-em" to a collie dog. They are the call to work.

Chapter 10 Examination

1. What should you do to get inside the door on your call?

2. What sort of things should you be sensitive to at the door that might keep you from entering the house?

3. If no one is at home when you call, what should you do?

4. When should you make an appointment before calling?

5. List the four types of calls from memory.

6. At your first call, what are some subjects of discussion to help you get acquainted?

7. How can you make visitors feel more comfortable in their early visits to the church?

8. What is a must if you are planning to teach a person about Christ?

9. What should you avoid when seeking to lead a person to Christ?

10. Give by memory the seven steps of an interview or call.

11. Give a brief explanation of each of these steps.

12. How can you deal with hard questions for which you have no ready answer?

11

DEVELOPING A STRATEGY FOR TEACHING THE LOST

". . . how I did not shrink from declaring to you anything that was profitable, and teaching you publicly and from house to house, solemnly testifying to both Jews and Greeks of repentance toward God and faith in our Lord Jesus Christ." Acts 20:20-21

There are basic principles that should be followed in teaching a person about Christ. Many methods have been presented by many different people. The following rules should be used: When we teach people, we should teach them with integrity; that is, the whole gospel plan should be covered, without omitting some parts. Often people teach only part of what Jesus asked people to do in order for them to become Christians. For example, poor teaching can result in a person's faith not being properly founded in Christ. A person may not be taught about repentance or a public confession of faith. A person may not be taught about Christian baptism as the scripture teaches. Those who are going to teach the lost about Christ ought to be sure that the plan they are following is Biblical and not twisted to meet some theological deviation from scripture.

It is important that a person use the Bible. The Bible should be used as the basis upon which all teaching is founded. The Bible should be used in order, not taking scriptures out of context, or from here, there, and everywhere.

One Bible book should be used, if possible, to avoid confusing the person being taught. The book of Romans is well adapted for this task. Its beautiful coverage of most theological issues that arise in conversion makes it a natural for this purpose.

The teacher may need to chain reference his Bible. Chain referencing one's Bible is easy and makes it possible for a person to open, teach from the Bible, and consistently follow an intelligent teaching plan. Often times people will become nervous when in the presence of someone they do not know very well, and even if they have the chain reference well memorized, they will need to rely on their margin references to tell them where to turn next.

C.S. Lovett gives twelve reasons why using a planned presentation is important.

1. It gives you a tremendous confidence that in turn produces a boldness.
2. You never have to grope for words for you know always what you are going to say next.
3. You have the advantage of knowing what to expect from the subject with whom you are dealing.
4. You can control the conversation.
5. You are forced to stay on the subject and work systematically toward the one goal of the subject's salvation.
6. You are free to analyze the subject and study him instead of having to plan what you are going to say next.
7. Your plan is one that Jesus has used to bring hundreds to Himself.
8. You can bring one to a decision much faster.
9. You are prevented from becoming confused.
10. The subject develops confidence in you because you know what you are doing.
11. You do not need a lot of Scripture verses to accomplish the task.
12. Your mind is freed from the stress of planning your next move, and you will find that you are able to keep in touch with the Lord as well as explain the steps.[1]

A number of Bible plans for teaching have been suggested by different soul winners. The following one has been developed out of over twenty years of experience in personal evangelism, and covers the important theological issues involved in a person becoming a Christian. It

---

1. C.S. Lovett, *Soul Winning is Easy*, (Grand Rapids, Michigan: Zondervan Publishing House, 1976), pp. 68-69.

is suggested that it be learned and followed carefully without deviation. Each part is given because it has a significant place in the teaching plan. The purpose is to teach a person with integrity. You will note that it was taken out of one Bible book with only one exception; that one scripture is read for comparison from I Corinthians to emphasize and explain a passage from Romans.

Many people have used a similar teaching plan called "The Roman Road to Salvation." This teaching plan is modified and different in some aspects, while similar in other areas. The following plan can be used with integrity to teach a lost person about Christ. It can be used verbatim, if you desire.

THE ROMAN ROAD TO SALVATION.

It used to be said that all roads lead to Rome. Rome became the builder of great highways. Roman roads, in some parts of the Roman Empire, still remain today that were built in the time of Jesus Christ.

There is another road that was built by Jesus Christ, Himself, and it is the road to salvation. The apostle Paul clearly outlines this road in the book of Romans, thus we call this the Roman road to salvation.

It begins in Romans one, where the writer says, "For I am not ashamed of the gospel, for it is the power of God for salvation to every one who believes, to the Jew first and also to the Greek."[2] The word gospel originally meant good news, good news about many different types of subjects. The Bible writer, Mark, apparently first used it to apply to the message of salvation through Jesus Christ. Scholars think he was the first to put it in print. The good news of salvation through Jesus Christ was of such a wonderful nature that it came to be known as "the gospel," the good news. The word was taken over by Jesus to refer to that work that He did for us; today the word gospel almost always has reference to the salvation offered by Jesus.

In this particular verse of scripture, it says that salvation is for those who believe, to Jews as well as Greeks. This included the whole spectrum of the Roman world for Greek was universally the language of the entire Roman world. Today salvation is for people throughout the

---

2. Romans 1:16.

whole world who believe and accept him.

Next note verses 18-20. Paul explains to us how we can know that there is a God. There are two evidences of God, the internal and the external witness. Verse eighteen says:

> For the wrath of God is revealed from heaven against all ungodliness and unrighteousness of men, who suppress the truth in unrighteousness, because that which is known about God is evident within them; for God made it evident to them. For since the creation of the world His invisible attributes, His eternal power and divine nature, have been clearly seen, being understood through what has been made, so that they are without excuse.[3]

A person must believe in Jehovah God in order to become a Christian. Salvation originated in God and until a person has a real understanding and belief in God, the creator of all things, then he is not ready to become a Christian. Verse nineteen indicates that God has manifested Himself "within" each person. This is what we call the internal witness. This explains why all cultures of man have gods. It is evident that there is a God and they have sought to find and worship this God. People just naturally have an innate awareness that there is a God. This is because God has manifested Himself "within" mankind. (At this point it would be well to ask the candidate for salvation if he believes in God. If he has had the feeling within himself that there just has to be a God who created all things, it is because God has shown Himself to him.)

The second point is, "for since the creation of the world His eternal attributes, His eternal power and divine nature, have been clearly seen, being understood through what has been made. . . ."[4] This is the external witness. Just looking at the stars and the heaven declare to us that there has to be a creator. It should be evident that there is a force to create and control all of this. God's power causes the stars and planets to move in their own prescribed realm. Looking at the beautiful sunsets, the beauty of nature, the flowers, the trees, the mountains and streams, speaks to us of God. Even one's own hand shows God's beautiful design; the very nature of a person's hands speaks of the fact that there

---

3. Romans 1:18-20.
4. Romans 1:20.

is a God. So we have the external witness, as well as the internal witness of God.

The passage goes on to discuss what happens to those who know God because of the internal and external witness, and yet do not accept Him or acknowledge Him as God. They became grossly sinful. (It is important at this point that the person acknowledge his faith in God.)

The next concept that is taught in this great book of Romans is that when man knew there was a God and did not accept Him as God, he became sinful. In fact, in the third chapter, it says:

> . . . as it is written, "There is none righteous, not even one; there is none who understands, there is none who seeks for God; all have turned aside, together they have become useless; there is none who does good, there is not even one. Their throat is an open grave, with their tongues they keep deceiving, the poison of asps is under their lips."[5]

A summary is given, ". . . for all have sinned and fall short of the glory of God."[6]

The Bible, it should be explained, is the record of the best people who have ever lived on the earth and how these people have sinned. Adam and Eve were the only full grown adults who were without sin, with the exception of Jesus Christ, and yet Adam and Eve who walked and talked with God in the garden, sinned and had their fellowship with God broken. Noah is another example. He was the savior of the whole human race, and yet Noah became drunk after they came out of the ark. Father Abraham, the ancestor of faith of all who believe today, told lies about his wife on at least two occasions. David, who was said to be a man after God's own heart, committed adultery and murder. (Unless the person will admit that he is lost and sinful, it is useless to continue teaching him.)

It says in Romans the sixth chapter, verse twenty-three, "For the wages of sin is death." Therefore, a person who is a sinner is dead, and he is separated from God. He can have no hope of salvation as long as he remains in this sinful condition.

Thus far, this hasn't been very good news, but the good news begins in verse twenty-four. Let us read:

---

5. Romans 3:10-13.
6. Romans 3:23.

> . . . being justified as a gift by His grace through the redemption which is in Christ Jesus; whom God displayed publicly as a propitiation in His blood through faith. This was to demonstrate His righteousness, because in the forbearance of God he passed over the sins previously committed; for the demonstration, I say, of His righteousness at the present time, that He might be just and the justifier of the one who has faith in Jesus. [7]

These verses explain God's process of working to bring sinful man back into fellowship with Him. Of course, as has been already shown, this fellowship can only be restored by faith, hope and love. When a person wishes to understand what becoming a Christian means, there are four words in this text that are very important.

The first is "justified." He speaks of a person being justified as a gift. The word justified has been explained to children for years as meaning "just-as-if-I'd not sinned." Certainly it is true when a person becomes a Christian that his sins are taken away as far as the East is from the West. They are buried in the deepest sea and remembered against him no more. Justification is not earned by a person being good enough, or righteous enough, but is a gift by grace. The word grace means unmerited or undeserved favor from God. This means that we don't earn it because we somehow become good enough to become Christians, but it is given as a gift. Justification is given by God's magnanimous nature, wishing to bless those who have faith in Him and submit to Him.

The third word that is often hard for a person to understand is the word, "redemption." The word redemption is a term taken from the slave markets of the apostles' day. It was quite common for one person, either through act of war or personal indebtedness to become the slave of another person. When one person was a slave to another, it was impossible for him to redeem himself, since all that he produced became the property of his owner. Therefore it was impossible that redemption should come of his own ability. Redemption often came through a wealthy friend, someone outside of the situation of slavery, paying the price of release. Redemption was purchased by someone outside, and so the apostolic writer tells us that redemption came by Jesus Christ who paid the price for our redemption. We could not redeem ourselves, so Christ did it for us.

---

7. Romans 3:24-26.

Another analogy can be made from the pawn shop scene today. A person needing money can take a valuable article and pawn it at a pawn shop. It then becomes the property of the pawnbroker. When the person returns to the pawnbroker to redeem that which was originally his, he is sometimes shocked to learn that it costs considerably more than what he originally received for it. So it is with sin; we did business with Satan and became his possession. When the time came for Jesus to redeem us, the price of sin was death. Jesus paid for our redemption by dying, a price many times greater than that which we received out of our willfulness. The thought of redemption is to buy back.

The fourth difficult word that is used is propitiation; it has the meaning of sacrifice. The Hebrew people understood propitiation well. Their long heritage of animal sacrifice had taught them that atonement was made through sacrifice. Jesus Christ, hanging on the cross, was the propitiation, sacrifice. Propitiation is a word that turns our eyes to the cross of Christ, for there He was the sacrifice for sin. The wages of sin was death. Jesus paid the wages of sin, that we might go free and have life eternal. This propitiation is found in His blood. Animal sacrifices could not permanently take away man's sin. Jesus could die for more than one man's sins because he was divine as well as human. If he had only been human, He could have only died for one man's sin. Jesus, the divine son of God, not just a man, but God, could die, and did die for all mankind.

All of this took place that God's righteousness might be demonstrated to us by setting guilty sinners free; not set them free without the price being paid, but that He would let them off after having paid fully the price of their salvation. Two concepts are united, "For the wages of sin is death, but the free gift of God is eternal life in Christ Jesus, our Lord." [8] Next turn to the fifth chapter, verse twelve of the book of Romans, which says, "Therefore, just as through one man sin entered into the world, and death through sin, and so death spread to all men, because all sinned — ."[9] So Adam brought sin into the world and sin and death spread to the whole human race, but verse eight of this chapter tells us, "But God demonstrates His own love toward us, in

---

8. Romans 6:23.
9. Romans 5:12.

that while we were yet sinners, Christ died for us."[10] So Adam brought sin, but Christ brought righteousness to us. How do we obtain this righteousness? The first step is shown in Romans 5:1, "Therefore having been justified by faith, we have peace with God through our Lord Jesus Christ, through whom also we have obtained our introduction by faith into this grace in which we stand; and we exult in hope of the glory of God."[11] Faith is a most important word to the seeker for salvation. How can we demonstrate faith? Often times at this point, the author will take off his wedding ring or take out of his pocket a piece of money, and ask the person if he knows what is in the hand. He can't see it, taste it, touch it, feel it, or smell it. None of the five senses will work upon this particular object. There is only one way that the person can know what is in the hand, and that is by faith. It has to do with the integrity of the person teaching them.

How can we know that we have been justified and have had propitiation, grace, and redemption applied to our lives? It is all tied up in the redeeming work of God. His integrity is involved. God, who cannot lie, has promised us salvation if we will believe in and submit to Him. Justification comes by believing God and then doing as God has asked us to do.

The next passage discusses getting into Christ.

> Therefore we have been buried with Him through baptism into death, in order that as Christ was raised from the dead through the glory of the Father, so we too might walk in newness of life. For if we have become united with Him in the likeness of His death, certainly we shall be also in the likeness of His resurrection.[12]

A powerful comparison can be made by reading I Corinthians 15:3-4, along with Romans 6:3-4. "For delivered to you as of first importance what I also received, that Christ died for our sins according to the Scriptures, and that He was buried, and that He was raised on the third day according to the Scriptures."[13]

The gospel is that Christ died, was buried, and rose again on the

---

10. Romans 5:8.
11. Romans 5:1-2.
12. Romans 6:4-5.
13. I Corinthians 15:3-4.

third day. The person coming to accept Christ is, according to Romans 6:4, "buried with Him through baptism," so we can learn through this passage that baptism is a burial with Christ. We are baptized into His death; we are buried with Him, we are raised from the dead through the glory of the Father. The person is not left in the waters of baptism, but is raised to walk in a newness of life. Christian baptism is a reenactment of the death, burial, and the resurrection of Jesus Christ. The promise of verse five is that if we have been united with Him in the likeness of His death, dead to sin, to the old way of life, to the old temptations, and pleasures, then we are raised to walk in a new life.

So again we have Romans 6:23, clearly before our eyes, "For the wages of sin is death, but the free gift of God is eternal life in Christ Jesus our Lord."[14] The responsibility then, as a new, born-again child of God, is to remain faithful. This is clearly displayed for us in Romans, the twelfth chapter.

> I urge you therefore, brethren, by the mercies of God, to present your bodies a living and holy sacrifice, acceptable to God, which is your spiritual service of worship. And do not be conformed to this world, but be transformed by the renewing of your mind, that you may prove what the will of God is, that which is good and acceptable and perfect.[15]

Since God has been so good, patient with us, and so merciful to us, it is our duty as Christians to be faithful and serve Him. We are not any longer to be worldly, giving ourselves over to the things of this world, but we are transformed by the renewing of our minds. This will be accomplished through a study of the word of God, through faithfulness in attendance at the church services, by prayer, and by being around the Lord's table. All of these things work together and help us to grow in Christ. The new Christian will be learning for the rest of his life what he should do in order to be well pleasing to God.

In summary, salvation is through the gospel, the good news from Jesus Christ. Salvation begins in knowing God and recognizing that we are sinners. As sinners, we need justification, grace, redemption and propitiation. As we believe in God, Christ and His promises, we submit

---

14. Romans 6:23.
15. Romans 12:1-2.

to Christian baptism into Christ. As Christians, we become living servants of Christ.

At this point one can ask the person if he believes in God and Christ's work. If the answer is yes, then the next logical question is, "Would you like to become a Christian?" If the answer is yes, then ask, "And now why do you delay? Arise and be baptized and wash away your sins."[16]

Always pray before and after giving this teaching. Prayer is as important as air. Prayer always goes along before, with, and after conversion.

---

16. Acts 22:16.

Chapter 11 Examination

1. Why is a planned presentation necessary in teaching a person about Christ? Our text lists 12. Give six from memory.

2. Using mainly one Bible book to teach an unsaved person is wise. Why?

3. Give the Scriptures from memory of the Roman Road.

4. What does the word "Gospel" mean?

5. How can we know there is a God? Give the text and its basic reasoning.

6. Define: justification, grace, redemption and propitiation.

7. Christian baptism is a reenactment of what events in Christ's life?

8. How is a Christian to live according to Romans 12:1-2?

9. What should you do immediately with a person who accepts Christ?

10. The teaching should always be closed with _____.

12

TEACHING A DENOMINATIONAL PERSON OF THE NEW TESTAMENT CHURCH

"Now I mean this, that each one of you is saying, 'I am of Paul,' and 'I of Apollos,' and 'I of Cephas,' and 'I of Christ.' Has Christ been divided?" I Corinthians 1:12-13

Jesus did build His church, Matthew 16:18, and the Bible does give a plan for it. The admonition of scripture is to follow the Bible plan, Hebrews 8:5. Many people today are looking for a real Bible-teaching church. Many are tired of the sectarian, denominational emphasis and want to get back to the basics of religion. Many are tired of the unbelief that has been disseminated through the pulpits of our land. This gives a New Testament church the opportunity to reach out dynamically to people who have quit going to church or who are on the verge of quitting the church because of its inconsistencies and compromise.

It has been estimated today that fifty percent of the people who attend churches do not know what is meant when one talks of the new birth or conversion. Therefore, we need to be ready and able to teach these people about the New Testament plan of salvation and plan for His church. In order to do this, there are several things that one must know.

First of all, he must understand what the New Testament church is all about. When a person understands what the New Testament church is all about then he must be so committed to that plan for the church that he can really get excited about it. An ounce of enthusiasm has been said to be worth one hundred pounds of knowledge. Christians, committed mind, body, soul, and resources to the movement to get back to the Bible and the teachings of the church, are world changers. If we cannot get excited about it, it is probably unlikely that we will get anyone else excited about it.

The soul winner needs to know what the Bible teaches about the church. This certainly is a big assignment. The chart on pages 142 and 143 will give you an idea of the basic teachings found in the Bible about the church, its origin, organization, names, its creed, memorials, discipline, finances, and purpose.[1] This outline can be duplicated and glued in front of the personal evangelist's Bible. It can be a ready resource to check when one wants to refer to some particular passage that deals with a subject that is important to the person that is being taught. In addition, a careful study of the scriptures on this chart will help prepare a person to teach another about the New Testament church.

Not only does the soul winner need to understand what the New Testament church is all about, but needs to understand something about church history as well. It isn't likely that we will solve many problems until we know the problem, how it started, how it grew, and what comprises the problem today. The study of history can be a real blessing to the person who wants to teach the denominational unsaved person and bring them to an understanding of the New Testament.

APOSTASY FROM THE CHURCH

The ecclesiastical system of Romanism developed gradually. No one man sat down and planned the apostate developments. Rather, one thing led to another. To grow this monster, unbridled ambitions and undisciplined imaginations became the mother of invention.

By the Third and Fourth centuries, ecclesiasticism was pretty well shaped up. Preachers were called priests. By 325, Metropolitans (later known as arch-bishops) were elected. At that time also, the bishops of Rome, Alexandria, and Antioch were called super Metropolitans or Patriarchs (later called Cardinals). By the Fifth century, Alexandria,

---

1. This chart has been around in many similar forms for years.

Jerusalem, Ephesus, and Constantinople had Patriarchs, but Rome had a Monarchial bishop (later called a Pope).

The rapidity with which apostasy introduced false doctrines even surpassed the development of ecclesiasticism. The Gnostics are the "Knowing Ones." They favored the Sadducees and, like them, corrupted the religion of God with pagan philosophies. The Ebionites, like the Pharisees of Jesus' day, were legalists. They introduced many Jewish elements into Christianity. The Monarchians were a sect that held peculiar ideas about the Godhead. Manichaeianism was a little Christianity, stripped of all reference to the Jewish religion, and filled with Persian pagan philosophy. The Montanists, Novationists and Donatists were reactionary parties against the rest. The Montanists held to visions, dreams, the prophetic office, and exciting religious services. With the Ebionites, they also held to the Premillennial view of a thousand years earthly reign of Christ. The Novationalists and Donatists held but one common thing with the Montanists, that of purging the church of worldliness, compromise, and human additions; for this, they were persecuted.

Beginning with the theory of "Holy Ghost Baptism," prophets visions, seasons of ecstasy, premillennialism, infant baptism, etc., many human doctrines were introduced.

Most of these doctrines were introduced during the period entitled "Formation of Catholic Doctrine." The doctrines formed at this period are for the most part accepted by both the Roman and Greek Catholic Churches (The Roman or Western and Greek or Eastern). The Romish church recognizes twelve more Councils that were held throughout the years, of which the Council of Trent is the most significant, because it was at this council that most of the doctrines now practiced by the Roman Catholic Church were formulated into crystalized dogmas and made "official" and binding.

The development of the Papal (political-religious) power kept pace with the growth of the ecclesiastical element and the introduction of heretical teaching. As early as the middle of the Third century, Cyprian advocated Papal primacy, which means Roman control of religion by political policies. By the Fourth century, the clergy of Constantinople, Alexandria, Jerusalem, Antioch, and Rome sought control of the remaining churches. In the fifth centruy, Augustine dreamed up the Papacy, which was developed during the later centuries; his "brain-storm" was published in a set of books called "City of God." In the middle of the Fifth century, Leo claimed authority over other Patriarchs. In 533, Emperor Justinian declared John II to be "Lord of the Church." In 600, Gregory I (first real pope, though not so called) organized his papal army and fought wars on behalf of the church. In 607, Emperor Phocas made Pope Boniface III "Head of all the churches."

The Papal States were organized when Pepin (in 756) and

141

The Church Revealed In The Scriptures

ORIGIN {
TIME—A.D. 30. Acts 2:1
PLACE—Jerusalem. Acts 2:5

FOUNDER—CHRIST—Matthew 16:18
FOUNDATION—I Cor. 3:11 and Eph. 2:19-20

ORGANI-ZATION {
HEAD—CHRIST—Eph. 1:22-23. "All Authority" Matt. 28:18. Legislation: Executive-Judicial
OFFICERS—Evangelists, Eph. 4:11; Elders, Act 20:17-28, I Tim. 3:1-7, Titus 1:5-9
Deacons, I Tim. 3:8-13, Acts 6:1-6
MEMBERS—Penitent Baptized Believers, Mark 16:16; Acts 2:41, 4:4, 5:14; Gal. 3:27
GOVERNMENT—Congregational, Acts 6:3-6, 13:1-3, 14:23; I Cor. 5:4-5; II Cor. 8:19
WORSHIP, Acts 2:42, 20:7 ONE Body, Spirit, Hope, Lord, Faith, Baptism, God. Division Carnal Romans 16:17-18 I Cor. 1:10-13; 3:1-3
UNITY, Acts 4:32; Eph. 4:5-6

The Gospel Only Isa. 62:2; Acts 11:26 I Peter 4:16; James 2:7

Of Individuals {
Disciples   Acts 6:1   - Learners
Saints   "   9:13 - Character
Brethren   "   6:3   - Relationship   Makes Christians Only   Acts 26:28-29
Christians "   11:26 - Ownership

Universal
Planner
Honor
Activity
Ownership
Character
Devotion to Christ

NAMES

Of Churches {
The Church   Acts 9:31
Church of God   I Cor. 1-2
Church of the first born   Heb. 12:23
Body of Christ   I Cor. 2:27
Churches of Christ   Romans 16:16
Churches of the saints   I Cor. 14:33
Christians   Acts 11:26

CREED { Jesus Christ
Preached— Acts 2:22, 8:5; II Cor. 11:4
Believed— John 20:30-31; Acts 8:12
Confessed—Matt. 16:16; John 1:49
I Tim. 6:12-13; II Tim. 1:12

Needs No Revision
Heb. 13:8, 7:25-28
I Cor. 1:24

THE LORD'S DAY

Set Apart	John 20:26	
Claimed	Rev. 1:10	
Observed	Acts 20:7	

MEMORIALS

THE LORD'S SUPPER

Instituted	Luke 22:19	Seal	I Cor. 11:25
Participation	I Cor. 10:16	Proclamation	I Cor. 11:26
Unity	I Cor. 10:17	Life Sustaining	I Cor. 11:30

DISCIPLINE

THE NEW The Only Rule of Faith and Practice: Gal. 6:16; Phil. 3:16; II Tim. 3:16-17
TESTAMENT Every New Covenant Command is an Ordinance.
Human Legislation is sinful. Matt. 15:9; Mark 7:1-12; I Cor. 4:6; Gal. 1:8-9; Rev. 22:18-19

FINANCES

Ordained— I Cor. 9:14; Gal. 6:6-8. How much? In Type - Heb. 7:1-10; Gal. 3:7-9
Admonished—I Cor. 16:2; II Cor. 9:6-10. Who? When? Why? How? {Matt. 23:23 {Matt. 5:20
Blessed— Acts 20:35; Luke 6:38; Luke 16:9; Matt. 6:19-21

PURPOSES

Preach the Gospel - Mark 16:15 **"ALL THE NATIONS"** Baptize Them - Matt. 28-19
Make Disciples - Matt. 28:19 Luke 24: 46-47 Teach Them - Matt. 28:20
Commit to Faithful and Able Men in Self-Governing, Self-Supporting, Self-Extending
Churches—II Tim. 2:2; Act 13;3-4; Jude 3

"Make All Things According To The Pattern" Hebrews 8:5

REQUIREMENTS FOR SALVATION

GOD'S PART
GRACE: Eph. 2:8-9; I Cor. 1:4; John 3:16
PREACHING: Mark 16:15; Acts 2:14; Acts 8:35; I Cor. 1:21

SINNER'S PART
HEAR: Matt. 17:5; Rom. 10:17
BELIEVE: Acts 2:37
REPENT: Acts 2:38; Acts 17:30-31
CONFESS: Rom. 10:10; Matt. 10:32-33
BE BAPTIZED: Acts 22:16; I Pet. 3:21
LIVE GODLY: I Tim. 6:11-16; Phil. 4:8-9; Gal. 5:21-22
HEBREWS 5:9

RESULTS OF SALVATION

JUSTIFIED: Rom. 5:1
SANCTIFIED: Acts 26:18
FORGIVEN: I John 2:12
RECONCILED: Rom. 5:10
REDEEMED: I Pet. 1:18-19
ADOPTED: Gal. 4:5
SAVED: Titus 3:5

No Book But The Bible!
No Creed But The Christ!
No Names But Those
   Divinely Given!
No Message But The
   Gospel!

Rev. 22:18-19
and I Cor. 4:6
No Subtractions
No Substitutions
No Additions

Charlemagne (in 774) made contributions of land to the Popes. These continued in the power of Popedom until taken away in 1870 by Victor Emmanuel and Garibaldi, and returned to Italy.

The Papacy, unable to prove Papal authority by the Bible, forged two documents. By these, they attempted to prove that Roman emperors gave temporal authority, as well as religious, to the pope. These two were "Donations of Constantine" and "Pseudo-Isidorian Decretals." However, even the Catholics now confess that they were frauds and not authentic — but only after they served their purpose of supporting the anti-Christ!

Nicholas I (858-867) first used these to great advantage in gaining for the Papacy great political power and prestige. The Cluniac Reform launched from the Cluny monastary, used these forgeries to enhance the Papacy. Hildebrand and Humbert, two Cardinals, also used Popes Leo IX, Nicholas II, and Alexander II as tools to develop the Papacy along the lines advocated in these documents. This led to the organization of the College of Cardinals, the purpose of which was to select the popes. Prior to this, popes had been placed in power by emperors.

Innocent III, using all of these advantages, developed the Papacy to its height (1198-1215).

The decline of the Papacy came when Boniface VIII undertook to maneuver political measures that he could not handle. As a result, he was dethroned and sent into exile by the king of France (Phillip the Fair). This led to the "Babylonian Captivity," so styled because the popes for seventy years ruled from Avignon, France. This in turn led to three different men claiming to be popes, two in Rome and one in France. This is called the "Papal Schism." This embarrassing situation was remedied only when the Council of Constance was called to depose the three contending popes and to install Martin V. By this time, the Papacy was so weakened that it could scarcely resist the oncoming Reformation.

At the beginning of the Tenth century, there was an element in the Roman Catholic Church objecting to its policies and practices. The Albigenses broke from it because of doctrinal differences. Later, the Waldenses broke from it because of both doctrinal and practical differences. A crusade launched against the Albigenses by the Papacy annihilated them. Great persecution waged against the Waldenses rendered them almost extinct.

In the fourteenth century, John Wycliff translated the Bible into the common tongue and instituted an era of learning. This "Morning Star of the Reformation" was followed by John Huss and Savonarola who taught the Bible and freely exposed much Catholic doctrine. Though martyred, their work resulted in a great discontentment against Catholicism. When, in 1517, Luther tacked his ninety-five theses on the Wittenberg, Germany Catholic Church door, all Germany, and later all the religious world, was set aflame either for or against Catholicism. Great efforts at reform were undertaken by such men as Luther and Melanchthon in Ger-

144

many, Zwingli and John Calvin in Switzerland, John Knox in Scotland, and Thomas Cranmer, Cromwell, and others in England.

From this Reformation, the Lutheran church of Germany resulted. In England, the Church of England came into being which in turn produced the Episcopal Church of America. The Congregational Church, called "Dissenters" and "Independents," broke from the Church of England as a result of the Puritan Movement. Due to a bogging-down of the religious life in the Church of England, the Wesley brothers produced the Methodist Church. Because of a formalizing of that denomination, the Holiness Agitation (a revival movement started by Finney, Moody, and others) produced the various Pentecostal and Holiness bodies. The Presbyterian group was started in Switzerland by John Calvin and in Scotland by John Knox. A desire for union on the part of the Presbyterians and the Congregationalists led to the formation of the United Brethren — the union failed. The Baptist bodies resulted from the Anabaptists (a word which means "re-baptizers").

Before leaving this period of church history, let us call attention to several additional facts: (1) There have been four successive divisions and healings of breaches between the Roman and Greek Catholics. The fifth division occurred in 1054 and has never been healed — nor is it likely that it will ever be. The main cause of it was over religious authority. (2) The Roman Catholic Church boasts that it is not divided like the rest of the religious bodies. That is both true and false. True, because when people differ from it, they are excommunicated ("boot them out"). And false, because there are exactly eleven other Catholic groups not including the Greek Catholics. (3) The crusades, ten in all, but seven Holy Land crusades, were mainly sponsored by and in the interest of the Catholic Church of Rome. They were designed for their own exploiting. (4) Against the Reformation, the Catholics warred with a Counter Reformation. They called the Council of Trent in order to effect a reformation in their own ranks and to systematize their doctrines in order to know what they did believe and teach. Ignatius Loyola organized the Jesuits, who soon gained control of educational centers, proselyted new members in other lands, instituted the terrible inquisition called the "Reign of Terror," and laid far-reaching plans in behalf of the Apostate Rome.

RETURN FROM APOSTASY TO THE APOSTOLIC CHURCH

What history calls the "Restoration Movement" is in reality a misnomer, because the church needs no restoring — it is perfect. When it gets into a condition that needs restoring, it no longer continues to be the church. Rather, people who have departed from the church need to return to it. This return "movement" resulted in many people being led out of "Mystery, Babylon the Great." It resulted in the formation of many congregations patterned after the New Testament order.

However, not all was good, for soon much of the "movement" stopped moving and stagnated. This stagnation produced three (groups). . . .

(1) One portion of the movement formed into what is known as the "Christian Church" or "Church of Christ." These churches are a loose-knit fellowship of conservative churches. They have an annual non-official meeting known as the North American Christian Convention.

(2) In conjunction with the Christian Church arose the Disciples of Christ denomination. Lines were hard to draw for a number of years, but now they are very clear. The main difference is that one group is for the organized Society and the other is against. Three things stand out in the development of the latter denomination. (a) All State Societies were developed in the eleven year period 1839-1850. (b) The six organizations from that date until 1919 were: American Christian Missionary Society (1849), Christian Women's Board of Missions (1874), Foreign Christian Missionary Society (1875), National Benevolent Association (1886), Board of Church Extension (1888), and Board of Ministerial Relief (1895). (c) All of these were dissolved in 1919 and reorganized into the United Christian Missionary Society. The denomination's headquarters are in Indianapolis, Indiana, at the present, with the official publishing house being located at St. Louis, Missouri, called Christian Board of Publication. . . .

(3) (The) Churches of Christ (non-instrumental) bind things of judgment (such as communion sets, Sunday Schools, tuning forks, pianos, etc.) upon Christians as though they were matters of faith. The writer is not referring to those who might have a definite conviction about the above named matter, but those who make them tests of fellowship to the exclusion of those who consider them aids and matters of judgment. . . .[2]

How can we successfully teach a denominational person about the New Testament church? Let's assume that we are now sitting in the home of a person who does not understand about the New Testament church. We have asked the person, "Would you like to understand about the New Testament church and its purity of doctrine in our world of confusion and sectarianism?" Of course, the person's response should be, "Yes." We would begin by opening our scriptures to II Thessalonians, the second chapter, which says:

Now we request you, brethren, with regard to the coming of our Lord

---

2. Burton W. Barber, "The Church Historically Traced." (Vega Beja Church of Christ, P.O. Box AJ, Puerto Rico 00764, 1982)

Jesus Christ, and our gathering together to Him, that you may not be quickly shaken from your composure or be disturbed either by a spirit or a message or a letter as if from us, to the effect that the day of the Lord has come. Let no one in any way deceive you, for it will not come unless the apostasy comes first, and the man of lawlessness is revealed, the son of destruction, who opposes and exalts himself above every so-called god or object of worship, so that he takes his seat in the temple of God, displaying himself as being God. Do you not remember that while I was still with you, I was telling you these things? And you know what restrains him now, so that in his time he may be revealed. For the mystery of lawlessness is already at work; only he who now restrains will do so until he is taken out of the way.[3]

This passage predicts that there would come an apostasy and that the lawless man, the son of the Devil would actually sit in the temple of God, saying that he was God and had the power of God. This apostasy had already begun in the church. Historically speaking, it is quite easy to trace the problems that came in the church. The church grew and became strong in Alexandria, Jerusalem, Antioch, Asia Minor, (this area originally centered in Ephesus and later in Constantinople) and Rome.

It was only natural that the smaller churches in the countryside would look towards the larger churches in the cities in times of need. In fact originally, within the church, the elders or bishops held one and the same positions, synonymous positions. As time passed one elder became more outstanding than another in the various population centers of the church. Thus, for example, in Alexandria the one outstanding elder from the group became known as "bishop" and he held just a little bit more authority than the lesser men (the elders) in the church.

It was only a process of time until surrounding churches from the countryside would look toward the larger church for authority and help in times of doctrinal or other types of crisis that would arise in the church. Therefore, one man came to have authority in various parts of the empire; there were area bishops. As time passed, there became five centers of the church. The center of Egypt was Alexandria; of Palestine, Jerusalem; of Syria, Antioch; of Greece and Asia Minor, Constantinople; and of Western Europe, Rome. With the Moham-

---

3. II Thessalonians 2:1-7.

medan invasion came the destruction of the church in Syria, Palestine, and Egypt, leaving two major religious apostasies of antiquity, the Greek Orthodox Church, and the Roman Catholic Church. Both bodies had what was predicted in the book of Thessalonians, a monarchal bishop, who later came to be known as the chief bishop of the church, or in Rome, the Pope or Holy Father.

Gradual deviations from the truth came. After authority was invested in one man or in a small group of men, then each new tradition that was incorporated into the church helped lead the church away from Christ. Another facet of this apostasy came even before the time of the monarchal bishop. The Emperor Constantine gave gifts to people to become Christians and made Christianity popular throughout the empire. Many pagans came into the church with their candle burnings, icons or idols, and many pagan practices.

Thus, gradual deviation from the truth came until the Lord and the apostles would have hardly recognized the church as it was in its apostasy. This apostate condition was recognized by the reformers who sought to return to the truth and reform the church of their day. They were ousted from the church for their efforts. They drew up their own bodies, which many times began to form their own traditions again.

Reformation or restoration of the church is very desirable and something that needs to continually be sought after if it is to be accomplished. So the effort today is to return to the Bible plan for the church, to restudy doctrinal issues in the light of scripture with good, competent scholarship. The goal is to return to clear teachings of scripture and to get away from the sectarian and denominational attitude that is in evidence everywhere.

Of course, this is only a brief description of what has happened, but will give the caller an idea as to the approach that can be used to teach others about the apostate condition found many times in churches today.

Briefly let us talk about "The Church Revealed in the Scriptures," on page 142. A brief explanation of this chart will help the person to realize that there is a genuine effort being expended by the church to return to the plan given in scripture. Note that Christ is the head of the true church, that He started one church, that He is the founder and head of the church and that this church began in Jerusalem.

After going through a careful discussion of "The Church Revealed in the Scriptures" chart, point out to the person that if he really wants a church of integrity, one that is seeking to return to the teachings of Jesus Christ — which teachings will judge us in the last day — that he has found it. The New Testament churches are doing all within their power to follow the teachings of the word of God. It could be styled, "the thinking person's church."

After making a summary of the teachings of the chart, it would be a good time to ask for questions or objections to what has been said from the person. Likely they will have many questions about things that they do not understand. The teacher can answer their questions about various teachings of the church.

Remember, in all of this teaching, do not condemn other churches or try to pass blanket judgment on all people, or any person from any of the various religious bodies. Indicate that it is not our goal or purpose to condemn, but simply to return to purity of doctrine. We want people to receive the blessings that come with knowing Christ, and His church as it should be and as it was originally planned by Him. He who knocks his competitor's product sells it for him. Do not bring up problems or even get into a discussion of doctrines of the various different churches unless forced to do so. For example, if a person says, "I am a Methodist," do not begin to pass out blanket condemnations of the Methodist Church, because many Methodists do not know what their church truly teaches. By condemning, one can establish them further in false teaching.

The simplicity of the New Testament Church will appeal to thinking people; share its sensible teachings with them. They will be happy you did so. Isn't it wonderful to have for our allegiance the Lord Jesus and truth? We have no denominational walls to maintain or man-made decisions to uphold, just the truth. It appeals to people.

The caller must never forget that salvation comes by a personal relationship with Christ, not church membership. Church membership comes because we are saved. Converts to Christ are not made by talking about "our church." The information of this chapter is given as background so the caller can understand what has happened to the church and the basis of the condition today.

Spend your time talking about Jesus. When a person is truly converted to Him they will naturally want to be a part of the New Testament Church. Time spent talking about or against other churches is almost always counterproductive.

Usually the person will agree that Christ has but one true church. You can then get back to talking about their submission to the Lordship of Christ. Jesus said, "And I, if I be lifted up from the earth, will draw all men to Myself."[4] Salvation comes in knowing Jesus. Saved people are a part of His church and are faithful to it. Saved people want to follow the Bible plan for the church.

Prayer is the source of unity and revival. Pray for the unity of Christ's body, the church.

---

4. John 12:32.

Chapter 12 Examination

1. Memorize Hebrews 8:5 and write it by memory.

2. What percent of people who go to church nationwide do not know what it means to be "born again?"

3. When was Christ's church begun? Give approximate year.

4. Who is the Head of Christ's church? Give a Scripture proof.

5. Give a brief outline of its organization. (See chart)

6. Give several Scriptural names used in the Bible for the church. (See chart)

7. What is the New Testament church's only creed?

8. What were the two oldest apostasies of the church that are still in existence today?

9. How can this material aid in leading a denominational person to Christ's church?

13

TEACHING THE CATHOLIC PERSON ABOUT CHRIST

"Let no one in any way deceive you, for it will not come unless the apostasy comes first, and the man of lawlessness is revealed, the son of destruction who opposes and exalts himself above every so-called god or object of worship, so that he takes his seat in the temple of God, displaying himself as being God." II Thessalonians 2:3-4

· The temptation one must resist in talking with the Catholic person is to attack their church doctrine or structure. These matters are certainly a problem, but the real problem is that the person doesn't know Jesus Christ as Lord and Savior. They can be taught for weeks about what is wrong with the Catholic Church and still not know what is right about Christ. Their problem is that they do not know Jesus as Lord. Keep that clearly in mind.

Too often the author has spent hours teaching them what was wrong with their church and found that before his feeble efforts, the person did not know what their church really taught in the first place. When they understood what their church taught, then they were committed to it because that was their church. Thus, with this type of person, the personal evangelist should begin teaching them carefully about salvation. The suggested plan from Romans is very helpful. A discussion of their church should come only after they have accepted Christ, and after they have raised some question about the church. It may then be necessary to delve into some aspects of the teaching. Be very careful that they do not side step the real issue, Jesus. If they can side step you on the basic issue of Jesus and get you to attack their church, then they will feel justified in avoiding the issue of Jesus as Lord of their lives.

The following material may be helpful as background material in teaching them after they have dealt with the issue of Jesus. However, be very careful that the issue of Jesus and submission to Him in obedience is settled first. When this has taken place, they may have questions about certain doctrines in the Catholic church.

As with teaching the denominational person, it is important that the teacher know about the Bible church. A knowledge of "The Church Revealed in the Scriptures" will be a key to the understanding of what the scriptures teach on this subject and will be an absolute necessity if we are to teach the Catholic person about the true church. Material that has been covered in Chapter XII on teaching the denominational person will apply here also.

The Catholic may want to talk about authority. Authority is really a big issue for them. Is the church the authority and giver of the Bible, or is the Bible the authority in the church? These are the two issues at stake. Either the Bible is the product of the church or the church is the product of the Bible. Either the church comes by the words of Christ and His apostles or the church gives us people like Christ and His apostles.

Two passages of scripture are favorites with the Catholic people to seek to establish the primacy of Peter. That is, that Peter was the authority over the church and Peter had the keys to do as he thought best through what they would feel would be the direction of the Holy Spirit.

The first of these passages of scripture is found in Matthew, the sixteenth chapter:

> And I also say to you that you are Peter, and upon this rock I will build My church; and the gates of Hades shall not overpower it. I will give you the keys of the kingdom of heaven; and whatsoever you shall bind on earth shall be bound in heaven, and whatsoever you shall loose on earth shall have been loosed in heaven.[1]

If a person were to read this passage in Greek he would be less likely

---

1. Matthew 16:18-19.

154

to misunderstand it than in the English text. The Greek text says, ". . . that I say to you that you are *Petros* (a stone or pebble)." Then goes on to say, ". . . upon this rock (*petra*) . . ."; the term *petra* means a large slab of rock, bedrock, in distinction to *petros*, a small stone. Jesus is not referring to Peter as the rock of the church, but He is referring to the statement that Peter had made in verse sixteen, "Thou art the Christ, the Son of the Living God," as the rock or foundation of the church. Peter is promised the keys to the kingdom of heaven, to bind and loose. If we are to understand this to mean that Peter could do as he pleased in giving doctrine, contradictory to what had been taught by Jesus and His apostles, we are out of order. For this same promise was given not only to Peter, but the rest of the apostles as well in Matthew, "Truly I say to you, whatever you shall bind on earth, shall have been bound in heaven, and whatever you loose on earth shall have been loosed in heaven."[2] The promise here is not that the apostles could do as they pleased, but that they would speak under inspiration. God would lead them in their words, that what they said would be reliable and directed from the throne on high.

Peter was given the keys to the kingdom. Keys are used to open things. He opened the doors of the kingdom for the very first time in the second chapter of Acts. He proclaimed the gospel message for the first time and three thousand people became Christians. The sixteenth chapter of Matthew certainly does not teach the primacy of Peter.

In the gospel of John, the twenty-first chapter, is another passage that is used to seek to prove that Peter was something special among the apostles. This passage of scripture says:

> So when they had finished breakfast, Jesus said to Simon Peter, "Simon, son of John, do you love Me more than these?" He said to Him, "Yes, Lord; You know that I love You." He said to him, "Tend My lambs." He said to him again a second time, "Simon, son of John, do you love Me?" He said to Him, "Yes, Lord; you know I love You." He said to him, "Shepherd My sheep." He said to him a third time, "Simon, son of John, do you love Me?" Peter was grieved because He said to him the third time, "Do you love Me?" And he said to Him, "Lord, You know all things; You know that I love you." Jesus said to him, "Tend my sheep."[3]

---

2. Matthew 18:18.
3. John 21:15-17.

Does this passage teach the primacy of Peter? Is Jesus trying to embarrass the other apostles that are standing around at this particular occasion? Is Jesus saying, "Peter, do you love Me more than these other apostles?" Or is He trying to show Peter that he must love Him more than he does the fishnets, boat, and the occupation to which he had returned? The command of Jesus had been quite clear, "Tarry in Jerusalem until you receive power from on high." But Peter said, "No, I go a fishing," and he returned to his occupation. Jesus was trying to teach Peter that he should love Him more than these physical things then he should be willing to teach and spiritually feed the people who are His flock. It is unlikely that Jesus would have ridiculed the other apostles — particularly John, whom He loved deeply — by saying that Peter was superior to them or was to be the chief apostle. Jesus was trying to show Peter's lack of faith, and his need to do as He had instructed them to do. Just the opposite is taught from what Catholics hope to understand.

Another interesting matter is that at the Council of Trent, the Catholic church wrote off Protestants as being lost, condemned and separated from the grace of God. Later at Vatican II, most of the Protestants were written back into the church. Opposite edicts were given, one writing the Protestants out of the church, the other writing the Protestants back into the church. These are conflicting and opposite edicts. Does this prove the infallibility of the church? No.

On the other hand, the sacred scriptures have been proven to be infallible and true, always reliable. As it was said about Jesus Christ in Hebrews 13:8, He is "the same yesterday, today, yes and forever."

Finally, since the church is His body, primary authority within the church is Jesus Christ and it is important in teaching a Catholic person that this point be made. Jesus is the authority in the church and He has priority over every other person, organization, or group of persons. All authority has been given to Jesus in heaven and on earth. Jesus has reminded us that in the last days, His words will judge us (John 12:47, 48). Therefore, the Bible authority, the words of Jesus Christ, and His apostles, must take priority over all other systems of mankind.

Like Jesus, we should pray for the unity of His followers upon the word of God.[4] The job cannot be accomplished without fervent prayer.

---

4. John 17:21.

Many Catholic people have been led to a personal relationship with Christ through our Bold Ones.

Chapter 13 Examination

1. What temptation must be resisted when seeking to lead a Catholic to Christ?

2. To teach a Catholic how should you begin?

3. What should be kept as the main issues of discussion?

4. Authority is a big issue with many Catholics. What two passages of Scripture do they use to show Peter was the first Pope?

5. Give a brief explanation of each of these texts.

6. The basic authority in the church today is _____.

14

THE BIG ISSUE WITH THE CULTS

"For if one comes and preaches another Jesus whom we have not preached, or if you receive a different spirit which you have not received, or a different gospel which you have not accepted you bear this beautifully." II Corinthians 11:4

Several of the cults have one foundational error in common and that is, they dishonor Jesus Christ. In teaching people in these cults it is necessary, right from the beginning to settle the issue of the nature and person of Jesus Christ. The cults that we might include in this group are the Mormons, the Jehovah's Witnesses, the Armstrongites, and the Moonies.

Each of these groups will confess that Jesus Christ is the Son of God, but the real issue at stake is do they believe that Jesus is God, the Son? There is a big difference between these two statements. These cults believe Jesus is a created being, lower than Jehovah, not eternal. Each of their views differ somewhat from the other, but each denies that Jesus is God, the Son. The Mormons believe He was created spiritually at the same time we were. The Jehovah's Witnesses believe that He is Michael, the archangel. Each will deny the trinity doctrine as taught by historic Christianity. The word "trinity" is not used in scripture and so probably the word "Godhead"[1] would be a better word, yet the word

---

1. Colossians 2:9.

159

"trinity" is not an unscriptural word, as the doctrine is clearly taught in scripture.

Any discussion with these groups will center in on this key issue of whether Jesus is actually God or not, and does God exist in the form of three persons, the Father, Son and Holy Spirit. Do these three work together in complete unity and harmony? It must be admitted from the beginning that the trinity doctrine is one of the most difficult in scripture. Nevertheless, it can be established quite conclusively that it is a scriptural doctrine. This is the most basic issue in dealing with each of these four groups.

If one can show that there are three persons called God in the New Testament, and then can prove that there is but one God, then one has proven the trinity doctrine.[2]

The Bible teaches that there is a person called the Father, who is God. "For when He received honor and glory from *God the Father*, such an utterance as this was made to Him by the Majestic Glory, 'This is My beloved Son with whom I am well pleased.' "[3] Since each of these religious groups admit that there is a person called God, the Father, it is not necessary to give extensive proof. To the Christian, one clear verse of scripture is enough to establish a point beyond reasonable doubt. Since there is agreement on this point among the groups in question, there is no need to belabor the question.

The real issue is whether Jesus is God, the Son. It can be conclusively demonstrated that there is a person called God, the Son. When Moses was talking to God at the time of the burning bush, he asked God to identify Himself, "And God said to Moses, 'I AM WHO I AM'; and He said, 'Thus you shall say to the sons of Israel, I AM has sent me to you.' "[4] This passage is readily admitted by the cults to be speaking about Jehovah. Since the word that is used for I AM is the Hebrew word, "Hayah" and since "Hayah" is the verb form of the word "YHWH," it is clear that this passage of scripture is identifying the person who is speaking as the eternally existent one, Jehovah God. We derive our word Jehovah from the verb "Hayah," to be, existence. In a discussion with the Jewish leaders, Jesus told them, "Your father

---

2. A line of reasoning followed by Walter Martin.
3. II Peter 1:17.
4. Exodus 3:14.

Abraham rejoiced to see My day; and he saw it, and was glad. The Jews therefore said to Him, 'You are not yet fifty years old, and have you seen Abraham?' Jesus said to them, 'Truly, truly, I say to you, before Abraham was born, I AM.' "[5] On this occasion, Jesus claimed that He was Jehovah — that He was God. The Jews understood Him to be saying this and so they responded, "Therefore, they picked up stones to throw at Him; but Jesus hid Himself, and went out of the temple."[6] There is only one conclusion that a person can draw from these clear passages of scripture, and that is, Jesus claimed that He was God. The cults have a most difficult time getting around these clear scriptures. Jesus is God.

A second proof that Jesus is God is found in the book of Revelation. We read, " 'I am the Alpha and the Omega,' says the Lord God, who is and who was and who is to come, the Almighty."[7] This passage is admitted by Jehovah's Witnesses and the cults alike as having reference to Jehovah God. Verse twelve of the same passage says,

> And I turned to see the voice that was speaking with me. And having turned I saw seven golden lampstands; and in the middle of the lampstands one like a son of man, clothed in a robe reaching to the feet, and girded across His breasts with a golden girdle. And His head and His hair were white like white wool, like snow; and His eyes were like a flame of fire; and His feet were like burnished bronze. . . .[8]

When he identifies the person who is speaking, he says, ". . . And the living One; and I was dead, and behold, I am alive forevermore, I have the keys of death and of Hades."[9] It is clear that the one who was the Alpha and the Omega and the Lord God Almighty is none other than Jesus Christ. The twenty-second chapter gives additional information about this. Jesus says, "Behold, I am coming quickly, and My reward is with me, to render to every man according to what he has done. I am the Alpha and the Omega, the first and the last, the beginning and the end."[10] And then, "I, Jesus, have sent My angel to testify to you these

---

5. John 8:56-58.
6. John 8:59.
7. Revelation 1:8.
8. Revelation 1:12-15.
9. Revelation 1:18.
10. Revelation 22:12-13.

things for the churches. I am the root and the offspring of David, the bright and morning star."[11] Jesus is clearly identified in these passages of scripture as being the first and the last. The Old Testament sums it up well, "Thus says the Lord, the King of Israel and his Redeemer, the Lord of hosts: 'I am the first and I am the last, and there is no God besides Me.' "[12] So, again the Bible affirms beyond any doubt that Jesus is God.

The cults often deny that the Holy Spirit is God. For example, the Jehovah's Witnesses say, "The Holy Spirit is not a person but an influence. There is no personal Holy Spirit."[13] The Bible speaks of the Holy Spirit as a person on many occasions. This person is said to be God.

> But Peter said, "Ananias, why has Satan filled your heart to lie to the Holy Spirit, and to keep back some of the price of the land? While it remained unsold, did it not remain your own? And after it was sold, was it not under your control? Why is it that you have conceived this deed in your heart? You have not lied to men, but to God."[14]

Here, this passage speaks of Ananias lying to the Holy Spirit and then turns around and says he had lied to God. Obviously the Holy Spirit here is spoken of as God. People do not lie to inanimate objects — a chair, a plant, or a stone — they lie to people. It is impossible to deceive an "influence," but it is possible to deceive a person. It would be impossible to lie to an "influence;" it is possible to lie to a person. The Holy Spirit is identified as a person; this person is said to be God.

The Book of Acts gives further information about the Holy Spirit and His nature.

> And while they were ministering to the Lord and fasting, the Holy Spirit said, "Set apart for Me Barnabas and Saul for the work to which I have called them." Then, when they had fasted and prayed and laid their hands upon them, they sent them away. So, being sent out by the Holy Spirit, they went down to Seleucia and from there they sailed to Cyprus.[15]

---

11. Revelation 22:16.
12. Isaiah 44:6.
13. *The Atonement Between God and Man*, (Watchtower), p. 210.
14. Acts 5:3-4.
15. Acts 13:2-4.

Here the Holy Spirit speaks, calls and sends — all the things that persons do, not "influences" or "inanimate objects." The Holy Spirit is a personality and this personality is called by scripture, God.

In conclusion, we must note that Timothy 2:5 says, "For there is one God, and one mediator also between God and men, the man Christ Jesus." So we have shown there are three persons, the Father, the Son and the Holy Spirit, all called God, and yet the Bible says there is but one God. We have conclusively proven the Godhead or trinity doctrine. We have not only shown the trinity doctrine to be true, we have also established that Jesus claimed to be equal with and one with Jehovah God.

There is much about the doctrine of the Godhead that cannot be understood by even the most brilliant of theologians. This is because we are studying God. If we could understand Him, we would be a god ourselves. Yet, by faith, we take the scripture at its word and recognize that Jesus is God, the Son. This is the real issue in talking with people in the cults and this information will be very helpful in dealing with the root problem that seems to be common to those who want to exalt themselves and pull down the Lord of glory.

It is not imperative that we understand all about everything. There are many things in which we believe that we do not totally understand. We believe that men went to the moon and yet do not understand many of the problems or the scientific data that was necessary in order to do this. We do not understand the full process of banking, and yet are content to place our money in the bank. We do not understand all the chemistry involved in drug making, and yet are willing to take drugs when prescribed by a competent physician. We live by faith.

We need to beware of those groups today who teach contrary, unscriptural teachings about the trinity and Godhead. Satan, from the very beginning, wanted men to be confused as to the nature and reality of God. He wanted man to exalt himself and think that he could become God. The scripture is clear there is one God and one mediator between God and man, Christ Jesus, our Lord.

The trinity doctrine is taught repeatedly in scripture. At the birth of Christ in Luke 1:35, the annunciation was given in the name of the Holy Spirit and the Most High and the Son of God. The trinity is mentioned at Jesus' birth. At Jesus' baptism, the Father spoke from heaven — the Holy Spirit descended in the form of a dove and Jesus was present in the water.[16] The Great Commission[17] was given in the name of the Father, the Son and the Holy Spirit. The apostle Paul concludes his letter to the church at Corinth in the name of the Father, the Son, and the Holy Spirit.[18] On many occasions we find the Bible says that God did something and then turns around and says Jesus did it and then says the Holy Spirit did it. Unless we understand the trinity doctrine, we find the Bible in serious conflict with itself. For example, the Bible says, "In the beginning God created. . . ."[19] In Genesis 1:2, it says, ". . . the spirit of God was moving . . ." and yet in Colossians it says, "For in Him all things were created, both in the heavens and on earth, visible and invisible, whether thrones or dominions or rulers or authorities — all things have been created through Him and for Him."[20] Other examples could be given where works are ascribed to the Father, the Son and the Holy Spirit, each in order. Only one explanation could be given and that is that the Father, the Son and the Holy Spirit work in complete harmony and unity. They are one God.

It is confusing to the person who does not carefully examine the whole scriptures how Jesus could make statements about not knowing the time or the hour of His second coming, and yet be God. It is hard to understand Jesus' limitations while in human form. Paul helps us to understand this problem.

> Have this attitude in yourselves which was also in Christ Jesus, who although He existed in the form of God, did not regard equality with God a thing to be grasped, but emptied Himself, taking the form of a bond servant and being made in the likeness of men.[21]

He limited Himself for a purpose. Jesus was here in the flesh; He did not know all things. Jesus did not have all power. Jesus had put off being God to become a man. This is the basis of the incarnation doctrine itself.

The soul winner must remember that the issue with the cults is: "Is

---

16. Matthew 3:16.
17. Matthew 28:19.
18. II Corinthians 13:4.
19. Genesis 1:1.
20. Colossians 1:16.
21. Philippians 2:5-7.

Jesus God, the Son?" The Bible affirms that He is. They affirm He isn't. Will we be guilty of receiving those who come preaching another Jesus? Will we receive those with ". . . a different spirit which you have not received, or a different gospel which you have not accepted?"[22]

One does not need to get off on the issues of the Mountain Meadow Massacre or polygamy or a number of other doctrines about the Mormons, or talk with the Jehovah's Witnesses about Hell or eternal punishment. One needs to simply stay with the issue of, "Who is Jesus?" It can be demonstrated conclusively that they are teaching a false doctrine about Jesus. An examination of the doctrine of the "Moonies," shows that Moon wants to dishonor Jesus and elevate himself. Each, in his order, seeks to exalt himself. Satan tempted Adam and Eve with the hope they could become gods. Satan promised man that he could become God if he would follow Satan. These groups come with the same lie that if you follow them and their teachings you can learn how to be God. This all is based in the Devil's lie that has been put forth to men from the beginning of time.

---

22. II Corinthians 11:4.

Chapter 14 Examination

1. The foundational error with the cults is what?

2. Show how one can establish the trinity doctrine by the New Testament. (Briefly)

3. Briefly, explain how Revelation 1:12-15,18; 22:12-13,16, as compared with Isaiah 44:6 show Jesus is God.

4. Is the Holy Spirit a personage? Give Scriptural proof.

5. Give at least three texts that say there is but one God.

6. Why did Jesus (i.e. God) not know everything while in the flesh?

7. Why not talk about the Mountain Meadow Massacre or polygamy with a Mormon?

8. The cults generally dishonor Jesus and exalt _____.

15

TEACHING THE MORMON

"But even though we, or an angel from heaven, should preach to you a gospel contrary to that which we have preached to you, let him be accursed." Galatians 1:8

Whenever false doctrine is found, people may be reachable for Christ. People are basically rational beings. The truth stands; error cannot stand the light of investigation. Such is the case with Mormonism: Mormon people can be won. We will be talking primarily about the Utah branch Mormons, which is by far the largest group today. Many Christian people have felt that it was impossible to reach these folk for Christ, because of their strange doctrines. Many times it has been impossible because of our lack of understanding of their position and teaching. Actually, the Mormon people are easier to reach than those from many denominational groups; the reason being — their doctrine is so clearly wrong when examined in the light of scripture. Mormonism, when examined in the light of the Bible, has many faults. One can teach an honest Mormon person and lead him to Christ.

The basic issue in teaching a Mormon is their view of Jesus. (See Chapter 14.) From the author's experience, the following teaching can be very useful in leading the Mormon out of error. There are four things that need to be done. The first is the necessity of establishing that the Bible is the word of God. Next a careful comparison needs to be made of Mormon scriptures with the Bible. Third, the teacher needs to examine what the Bible says about prophets. Was Joseph Smith a prophet? And fourth, we need to examine Mormon doctrine in the light of sacred scripture.

THE BIBLE IS ACCURATE

The Mormon people have a basic mistrust of the Bible. This mistrust probably stems from the Articles of Faith of the Latter Day Saints Church. These Articles of Faith are thirteen in number. The eighth article of faith is: "We believe the Bible to be the word of God as far as it is translated correctly. We also believe the Book of Mormon to be the word of God."[1] This statement while not really inaccurate, leaves an inference that is misleading, and that is that the Book of Mormon is much more accurate than the Bible. The translation of the Bible is questioned.

Joseph Smith, Jr. made the statement that the Bible was inaccurate, "I believe the Bible as it read when it came from the pen of the original writers. Ignorant translators, careless transcribers, or designing and corrupt priests have committed many errors."[2]

Another Mormon scholar made a similar accusation against the Bible's accuracy. A son of Joseph Fielding Smith, recent prophet of the Latter Day Saints Church, made the following statement.

Scholars do not deny that the original text of the Bible has been corrupted. Truths have been removed to preserve tradition. Faulty translations and omissions of phrases and clauses have resulted in confusion.[3]

Another quotation says:

The early "Apostate Fathers" did not think it was wrong to tamper with

---

1. *Pearl of Great Price,* The Articles of Faith, No. 8.

2. B.H. Roberts, ed., *History of the Church of Jesus Christ of Latter Day Saints,* Vols. 1-6: *Period I. History of Joseph Smith, The Prophet,* by Joseph Smith; Vol. 7: *Period II.* From the Manuscript History of Brigham Young and Other Original Documents; 7 Vols., 2nd ed. (Salt Lake City, Utah: Deseret News Press, 1963), 6:57.

3. *Religious Truths Defined,* p. 337, cited by Jerald Tanner and Sandra Tanner, *Mormonism — Shadow or Reality?* (Salt Lake City, Utah: Modern Microfilm Co., 1964), p. 64.

the inspired scripture. If any scripture seemed to endanger their view-point, it was altered, transplanted, or completely removed from the Biblical text. . . . Such mutilation was considered justifiable to preserve the "purity" of their doctrines. [4]

Even the Book of Mormon claims that the Bible has been tampered with and changed.

> . . . for behold, they have taken away from the gospel of the Lamb many parts which are plain and most precious; and also many covenants of the Lord have they taken away. And all this have they done that they might pervert the right ways of the Lord, that they might blind the eyes and harden the hearts of the children of men.[5]

If a person might still be in doubt about Joseph Smith's teaching in regard to the inspiration of scripture, they should compare the *Inspired Version of Holy Scriptures*[6] with the Bible that most Christian people use today. Joseph Smith did what he felt was necessary to straighten out the Bible, correcting it, so that it could be relied upon. In fact, he made an estimated four thousand changes between the King James Version of the Bible and his Inspired Version. Many verses are added to the book of Genesis. The Song of Solomon is completely taken out of scripture. Joseph Smith took pen in hand to add to the Sermon on the Mount, the great sermon of Jesus Christ. This is confirmation of his view that the Bible had been revised and changed from what was written and used by Christ. He certainly felt many truths had been removed and that the Bible wasn't accurate as it had originally been written. It was necessary to change and revise it to get it right.

In order to teach a Mormon, one must first establish the accuracy of the Bible. This can quite easily be done in our day of modern scholarship. First, let's talk about the accuracy of the Old Testament Scriptures. Up until 1947, the oldest complete copy that we had of the Old Testament scriptures was dated in the year 1010 A.D. We had a partial manuscript called the Leningrad Codex that dated in the year 916.

---

4. *Religious Truths Defined*, p. 175, cited by Jerald Tanner and Sandra Tanner, *Mormonism — Shadow or Reality*, p. 64.

5. The Book of Mormon, I Nephi 13:26b-27.

6. Joseph Smith, Jr., *Inspired Version of the Holy Scriptures*, a new corrected edition, (Independence, Missouri: Herald Publishing House).

Therefore, it was easy for Joseph Smith to say that the Bible had many truths removed from it, because there was such a gap between the time the Old Testament writers wrote and the dates of the oldest copies of scripture then known.

Unfortunately for Jospeh Smith and the Mormon Church, the Dead Sea Scrolls were found between 1947 and 1950. Over three hundred copies of Old Testament books were found among them. These copies were dated by competent scholars from about 65 B.C. to as early as 225 B.C.[7] The Dead Sea Scrolls established the fact that our Old Testament Scriptures had not been changed from their basic essence. In fact, the Old Testament scriptures were handed down through the centuries with remarkable accuracy. It is not true that "many plain and precious truths had been removed" from the Old Testament scriptures. Removal of truths by ignorant scribes and designing transcribers was simply the figment of the imagination of Joseph Smith and other Mormon theologians. We have many copies of our Old Testament that were written significantly before the time of Christ. Jesus and His apostles placed their stamp of approval on the Bible that they had in their day, which is the same as the one that we have in our day. How thankful we should be to live in the period following this wonderful discovery.

When we examine the evidence for our New Testament scriptures, it is easily as conclusive as that in regard to the Old Testament scriptures. The earliest written fragment, to the author's knowledge, is that mentioned by Professor Jose O. Callaghan, Pontifical Biblical Institute, Rome. He makes the statement that there are nineteen tiny scraps of papyrus of Saint Mark that have been dated in the year 50 A.D.[8] Of course, this is not a copy of our whole scriptures, but it gives the chance to check on one of the earliest written books in our New Testament. The gospel of Mark could have been written as late as 47 A.D. and if so there are only three years between the time it was written and that which we have as a spot check on it in nineteen places.

The next evidence for the accuracy of our New Testament Scriptures is the Chester Beatty Papyri. It contains portions of the gospels,

---

7. A very fine book that discusses the significance and importance of the Dead Sea Scrolls is the book by William Sanford LaSor, *The Dead Scrolls*, (Chicago: Moody Press, 1962).

8. William S. McBirney, *The Search for the Twelve Apostles*, (Wheaton, Illinois: Tyndale House Publishing Company) p. 251.

Acts, the Pauline Epistles, Romans from 5:17 onward, Hebrews, I and II Corinthians, Ephesians, Galatians, Philippians, Colossians, and I Thessalonians. The book of Hebrews stands next to Romans. It contains the middle third of the book of Revelation from 9:10-17:2. This again gives us an early check on the accuracy of the Bible in many different places. These fragments have been dated between 150-250 A.D. by some scholars. H.S. Miller gives a fine description of these manuscripts.[9]

The next evidence for the accuracy of our New Testament Scriptures is the Bodmer II Text of the gospel of John. It is commonly referred to as P. 66, because it was written on papyrus — the sixty-six indicating the place that it has in the catalog of papyrus manuscripts. This fine copy of the gospel of John has been dated in the year two hundred. It is easily readable and establishes the unchanged nature of this gospel. It was written within 125 years of the time the apostle John originally wrote it.

There are four full copies of the New Testament Scriptures of great significance. These also are in Greek. There is the Sinaitic Manuscript that is dated in the year 340. It contains the whole New Testament Scriptures.

The Vatican Manuscript, also written in Greek, in about the year 325-350 contains the whole New Testament. The third is the Alexandrian Manuscript, dated around 450, which has almost a complete New Testament. These give us checks on the New Testament Scriptures and demonstrate that they have been transmitted accurately.

There are nearly four thousand Greek manuscripts of the New Testament Scriptures that come from all over the Mediterranean world. These have been diligently and carefully compared. After checking all of these manuscripts, no significant doctrinal issue can be raised because of textual problems. Isn't it wonderful and amazing that we can rely on our Bible as being authentic and uncorrupted? It is as Jesus Christ, Himself, said, "For truly I say to you, until heaven and earth pass away, not the smallest letter or stroke shall pass away from the Law, until all is accomplished."[10] And His statement in John, "And the

---

9. H. S. Miller, *General Biblical Introduction*, (Houghton, New York: The Word Bearer Press, 1959), p. 201.
10. Matthew 5:18.

Scriptures cannot be broken."[11]

The next step is to demonstrate the many problems with Mormon scriptures. Unfortunately the Mormon scriptures have not been transmitted with the same integrity as the Bible. Even though these "scriptures" are relatively modern, and we have copies of the original editions available of the Book of Mormon and the Doctrine and Covenants, we find that they have been greatly changed and revised to suit the needs of the church today. If proof is desired, check such books as *Joseph Smith Begins His Work,* volumes I and II, published by Wilford Wood, of Bountiful, Utah. These are reproductions of the original Book of Mormon and the Doctrine and Covenants.

A comparison of volume I with the Book of Mormon today will show that there have been 3,913 changes between the original edition and the present Book of Mormon. This amounts to about seven changes on each side of each page throughout the work. This is very devastating information when we realize that the original translation of the Book of Mormon was claimed to have been done by the gift and the power of God. The mistakes then, must be blamed on God if it was translated by His power.

In examining the Doctrine and Covenants, much more serious evidence is seen of corrupting and changing of the original text. The Doctrine and Covenants is a book of about the same size as the New Testament; yet, between the original edition and the current edition, there are 2,786 changes, including at least twenty doctrinal issues. The changes are complete and throughout. Some portions of the text are almost unrecognizable as compared with the original text. This is very confusing to the average person in the light of the statement of section 1 of the Doctrine and Covenants.

Search these commandments, for they are true and faithful, and the prophecies and promises which are in them shall all be fulfilled. What I the Lord have spoken, I have spoken, and I excuse not myself; and though the heavens and the earth pass away, my word shall not pass away, but shall all be fulfilled, whether by mine own voice or by the voice of my servants, it is the same. For behold, and lo, the Lord is God, and the Spirit beareth record, and the record is true, and the truth abideth forever and ever.[12]

---

11. John 10:35.
12. Doctrine and Covenants 1:37-39.

If this statement is true, why was it necessary to change and revise these revelations? Were they really given by God? For additional information in regard to this subject, see the book, *The Bible and Mormon Scriptures Compared*, by Charles A. Crane, College Press, Joplin, Missouri, 1983.

The third thing that needs to be done in dealing with Mormon people, to lead them to Christ, is to look at what the Bible has to say about prophets. Zechariah 13:1-3 teaches that after the time that Jesus came and lived and did His work, there would be no more prophets. If a person claimed that he was a prophet, then he spoke lies in the name of Jehovah.

Jesus said, "Beware of false prophets that come to you in sheep's clothing, but inwardly are ravening wolves."[13] Why would Jesus warn about false prophets if there was no possibility of having such? Jesus, in another place, said:

> Not everyone who says to Me, "Lord, Lord," will enter the kingdom of heaven; but he who does the will of My Father who is in heaven. Many will say to Me on that day, "Lord, Lord, did we not prophesy in Your name, and in Your name cast out demons, and in Your name perform many miracles?" And then I will declare to them, "I never knew you; depart from Me, you who practice lawlessness."[14]

Jesus indicated many people would come claiming to be prophets, and that He would have to declare that He did not know them. This passage goes on to give the illustration of the wise man who built his house upon the rock, who heard the words of Jesus Christ and did them and the foolish man who heard Christ and did not obey.

Jesus again warned, "For false Christs and false prophets will arise and will show great signs and wonders so as to mislead, if possible, even the elect."[15] Jesus was very clear in warning us that false prophets would come into the world. The apostle Paul also warns:

> But even though we, or an angel from heaven, should preach to you a gospel contrary to that which we have preached to you, let him be ac-

---

13. Matthew 7:15.
14. Matthew 7:21-23.
15. Matthew 24:24.

cursed. As we have said before, so say I again now, if any man is preaching to you a gospel contrary to what you have received, let him be accursed.[16]

The beloved apostle, John, said:

Beloved, do not believe every spirit, but test the spirits to see whether they are from God; because many false prophets have gone out into the world. . . . We are from God; he who knows God, listens to us; he who is not from God does not listen to us. By this we know the spirit of truth and the spirit of error.[17]

When a person begins to check the claims of Mormonism, he often will hear the words, "Foul play," used, that we should not question or criticize other people's religion. Yet the advice of this dear apostle was that we are to test the spirits to see if they are of God. The truth is never hurt by investigation, but error is. The apostle John teaches that the way to check supposed prophets is to compare their teachings with the New Testament writings. This is the test that will be used in the following paragraphs to answer the question, "Does their teaching and the Bible's match?"

The Mormon church teaches false doctrines about many things.[18] The first issue that should be discussed is the doctrine of God. The Mormons believe that God is an exalted human and that humans can be exalted to become God. Actually, they are not monotheistic, but polytheistic, believing in many gods.

The Mormon church teaches false doctrines about Jesus Christ, i.e., that Jesus Christ is a created being, i.e., that Jesus Christ was begotten by the Father, God, coming down and sleeping physically with Mary.

The Mormon church practices the Lord's Supper, contrary to the teaching of scripture, using water in the communion cup, rather than the fruit of the vine as Jesus authorized in Matthew 26:29. It is interesting to note that the Mormon church's own scripture, the Word of Wisdom from Section 89:5-6, of the Doctrine and Covenants, teaches

---

16. Galatians 1:8-9.
17. I John 14:1,6.
18. See the book, *The Bible and Mormon Scriptures Compared,* Charles A. Crane, (Joplin, Missouri: College Press, 1983), pp. 68-104.

that the Lord's Supper is to be observed with the fruit of the vine.

The Mormon church has many high priests, rather than just one. There are literally thousands of high priests running around the country. This is contrary to the very concept of the high priesthood, listed in scripture in the teaching of the book of Hebrews, the fifth through the eighth chapters.

The Mormon church teaches baptism for the dead, teaches heavenly marriage, teaches that Jesus, and salvation through Jesus Christ was preached by Adam, Enoch, Noah, Abraham, and others. The Mormon church teaches that some races of people are cursed of God and are inferior to others. The Mormon church has advocated polygamy almost from its beginning and even today, physical polygamy is not endorsed, but spiritual polygamy or celestial marriage to many different women is encouraged. The Mormon church's doctrine of exaltation would mean that Jesus would have to have been married. This has been and is still being taught by many people within the church.

The Mormon church teaches that the ministry should not be paid. This also is contrary to the teachings of the apostle Paul in I Corinthians.

> Do you not know that those who perform sacred services eat the food of the temple, and those who attend regularly to the altar have their share with the altar? So also the Lord directed those who proclaim the gospel to get their living from the gospel.[19]

Finally, in spite of the fact that the Bible teaches that both elders and deacons are to be married men with children, the Mormon church persists in ordaining young fellows from twelve to nineteen years of age to the office of deacon and elder, respectively. The book, *The Bible and Mormon Scriptures Compared*, (College Press Publishing Company) again will be a great help to those who wish to work with Mormons.

After teaching the Mormon these four things: the Bible is accurate, Mormon "scriptures" are not accurate, what the Bible says about false prophets, and the many false doctrines of the L.D.S. Church, then the Mormon needs to be taught the "Roman Road to Salvation." See Chapter 11 for that information.

When a person has finished this teaching, it would be helpful to refer

---

19. I Corinthians 9:13-14.

back to Chapter 11, "Teaching the Denominational Person About Christ." Use the chart, "The Church Revealed in the Scriptures," as a means of demonstrating to the Mormon person that there is a church in the world today and this church has been and can be restored to the Bible plan. This church does not have all the traditions and corruptions that come when we begin to rely upon men and their word.

The conversion of a Mormon to Christ may take several years. Help them begin to think for themselves; if they begin to think and check the facts — conversion will not be too far away. Pray for the whole Mormon church, that it will turn from its heresy to the Church of the living God. L.D.S. people can be led to Christ. Several hundred have been by the author and the Bold Ones. In a recent month three L.D.S. people came to Christ. The above approach has proven quite successful in so doing.

A WORD OF CAUTION

The apostle warns, "Knowledge makes arrogant, but love edifies," I Corinthians 8:1. There is a real and serious danger that we only prepare so we can "put down" L.D.S. people. Such an attitude will not be fruitful for our Lord.

It is only love that gives us the right to share with any Mormon person our faith. They will not listen to any other approach and should not. The truth, shared in love, may produce in them an initial response of frustration and anger. Yet, when we have the Spirit of Christ we will persist in being kind and loving.

It is necessary to show the L.D.S. person the error of the Mormon system. This will take a lot of careful, prayerful, research on your part. But remember information without love is dead.

Several things must be in your own life before you are ready to share with a Mormon friend.

1. Godliness. A complete surrender of your life to Christ.

2. Prayer. Trusting that God will work through you.

3. Friendship. This must be genuine. It may take years to earn the right to be heard.

4. Patience. To share too much too soon can be offensive. Help them to think. When that has happened they are on their way to Christ. Few L.D.S. persons have ever come to Christ quickly.

5. Truth. We are in search of truth.

Therefore, the material in this book is to be used with caution. When you are ready to share in love, begin by opening a conversation with a Mormon friend. Share patiently. Many of the L.D.S. people whom the author led to Christ took as much as five years.

We need to remember that L.D.S. people are not the enemy, but are victims of the enemy. What they need to hear first is the music of the gospel lived out in our lives. Then they will be ready to listen to the words of the gospel.

May God Bless in your efforts to share our Lord.

Chapter 15 Examination

1. Why have many churches been so poor at winning Mormons to Christ?

2. Why are Mormons reachable for Christ and often quite easily?

3. The basic issue with the Mormon is what?

4. What do Mormons believe about the Bible?

5. What is Joseph Smith's translation of the Bible called?

6. To teach a Mormon, one must do what as the first step?

7. How can you prove the Bible has not been changed?

8. About how many ancient, handwritten, Greek manuscripts of the New Testament are there in existence today?

9. About how many changes are there in the Book of Mormon and the Doctrine and Covenants, between original and the present editions?

10. What do Mormons believe about God?

11. What do Mormons believe about Jesus?

12. What five things should be in your life if you are to lead a Mormon to Christ?

16

DEVELOPING A PROSPECT LIST

"The Lord is not slow about his promises, as some count slowness, but is patient toward you, not wishing for any to perish but for all to come to repentance." II Peter 3:9

One of the problems that most churches face, especially small churches, is finding an adequate number of prospects. Small churches across the country report, "We just don't know of anyone who would be interested in becoming a part of our church."

Unless the church is in an area where there are no people, there should be prospects all around them. It is simply a matter of finding the prospects from among the people who live in the area where the church is situated.

AN IN-CHURCH SURVEY

Prospects can be recruited from member families. This can be done through an in-church survey. The Sunday School Superintendent, preacher, or other church leader can visit each adult class and request that each member write down four people who might be prospects for the church. These should be people that they would like to see become members of the local body. You could ask the people not only to write down names, but write them in the order of interest that they might show in the church. The person who writes the card can supply the addresses and possibly even the phone numbers of these people.

The person taking the survey should furnish cards to the class members. The class members can then list those that they would like to see won to Christ. Usually from a fairly small church, one hundred prospects can be found in such a manner. It is helpful for the person who gives the name of someone that he would like to see come to Christ, to place his name on the back of the card. If he seems at a loss to think of four families or four people that might be prospects, ask him to look for lost family members: moms, dads, kids, aunts, uncles, lost neighbors, or lost people that he works with on the job.

BIBLE SCHOOL SURVEY

A second means of finding prospects is from the Bible School enrollment. Almost all Sunday Schools have children who attend, but their parents do not. These parents are prime prospects. It is quite simple to take a census within the Sunday School to find the non-Christians. Ask the students who are in attendance to list friends they would like to see come to Sunday School. Send cards to invite them or call on them in their homes. From the average Sunday School, fifty to one hundred prospects can normally be found.

SILENT ROLL CALL CARDS

A third means of finding prospects within the church is the silent roll call cards. Silent roll call cards are an easy means of keeping track of guests who visit the church, who otherwise might be overlooked. Most church pews have a place on the back of them where silent roll call cards can be kept. It is good to have a time in each church service where a silent roll call card can be held up, with the request that every person in attendance fill one out.

The person in charge of visitation evangelism in the church should go through the cards right away on Monday. The first-time visitors should be called on early in the very first week after they came to church.

NEWCOMERS

A fourth means of finding prospects is to keep track of newcomers to the community. Many communities have an organization called Welcome Wagon. Welcome Wagon surveys all of the new people in the community and provides merchants with a list of all of these new people. If someone from the church can get the list that is provided for merchants who support Welcome Wagon in the community, it is a source for finding out who the new people are who have moved into the community. If Welcome Wagon cannot be used, then someone who works for the water company, gas company, phone company, the school district, or the electric company can get a list of all the new people who sign up for these services.

New people who come into the community can be placed on the church mailing list for the church newsletter for four weeks. At the end of four weeks, a call is often welcomed. It is also possible to send letters of welcome to these new people, after four weeks of having received the church newsletter.

HANDOUTS

The fifth idea is the use of brochures as handouts. These brochures can be left in places of business around town and can be used to hand out to homes within the community. They can be used as mail outs with all correspondence from the church and can be given to church members to spread far and wide throughout the community. This type of brochure is not a tract, but simply advertising, telling about the things that the church offers.

The community can profitably be covered every six months with these brochures. It is a good way to let people know about the church. One might wonder why every six months is suggested. People move so regularly in the United States today, that after covering the city, the need arises to cover it again. Usually new prospects will be found each time. Even if a person has not moved, often a crisis will have arisen in his life in the meantime and he will be more receptive to a message from the church than he was even a few months before. These hand-outs can be of great benefit to the church.

After the church has produced a brochure, they can be mailed to new people in the community, new arrivals, people that we have mentioned in previous sections. These same brochures can be passed out at work, and at school. Most businesses have found that advertising pays big dividends. Most advertising will continue to bear results, even as much as two years after it has been done.

A RELIGIOUS CENSUS

A sixth method that has been used to acquire prospects is a religious census or a house survey. Dr. Paul Benjamin offers a very fine form for surveying.[1] A sample form that can be used is shown on page 183. This card can be used by your church. It is not necessary to change it at all as Dr. Benjamin has given permission to any who wish to use it. These cards can be printed up by a local printer or on the church's mimeograph. Surveyors can go around the community, asking the appropriate questions, and finding the people who are prospects. One such survey taken in the Ogden, Utah, area turned up more than seven hundred prospects in one day. In another area of suburban Salt Lake City, four hundred prospects were found in one day by using the religious census method. So this is an excellent way to find prospects.

INSTITUTION VISITATION[2]

A seventh means of acquiring prospects is institution visitation. While calling in the hospital upon members or families and friends of the church, it is normal to ask about other people in the hospital who might

---

1. Dr. Paul Benjamin, *How In The World*, (Lincoln, Illinois: Lincoln Christian College Press, 1973), p. 26.
2. Matthew 25:36 ". . . I was sick, and you visited me."

WITNESS-SURVEY

Hello, I'm _____
I'm (We're) from the _____ Church. I'm (We're)
making a religious survey of the families in our area because
we want to serve others better. Will you please help us by
answering a few brief questions?

Street _____ Number _____

City or Suburb _____ Date _____

1. Are there any children or young people living here?
Age _____ Grade _____ What are their names?
_____
_____
_____

2. What is their last name?

3. Do they regularly attend Sunday School?
YES _____ NO _____
If "no," Would you consider permitting
then ask: them to attend our school?
YES _____ NO _____
If "yes," Do they need transportation?
then ask:
YES _____ NO _____

4. Are you attending church anywhere now?
YES _____ NO _____
If "yes," Which one?
then ask: (Specific church & community)

How often do you attend:
Once a week? _____ Once a month? _____
Once a year? _____
Are you a member? YES _____ NO _____

5. Is your husband/wife (cross out incorrect word) attending
church anywhere? YES _____ NO _____
If "yes," Which one?
then ask: (Specific church & community)
How often does (he/she) attend:
Once a month? _____ Once a year? _____
Is (he/she) a member? YES _____ NO _____

6. Are there other adults living here?
Information _____

7. What is the family name at this address?
_____

8. Would you be interested in a home Bible study group?
YES _____ NO _____

9. Would you be interested in a Bible correspondence
course?
YES _____ NO _____

10. May I (we) inquire what you believe about Jesus Christ?
_____

Note: Here may be the best place to share your own
testimony.

Not at home _____
Vacant house _____
Not responsive _____
Information refused _____
Responsive _____
Other _____

Name of surveyor _____

LCC Press, Box 178, Lincoln, Illinois 62656

183

be sick, or friends of your members from the community who are there. While visiting, it is appropriate to pray with folks who do not have a church home. Most hospitals list those who have no religious preference and just a short visit by a church member and a short prayer is often appreciated by these folks. Institution visitation engenders good will and will bring new folk to the church services. While visiting in the hospital, it is possible to find out where they live and to stop by for a visit at home after they have recuperated from their hospitalization. Not only hospital visitation, but nursing home visitation is a way to engender good will and to find out about families in the community.

DAILY VACATION BIBLE SCHOOL

An eighth means of finding prospects is that of Daily Vacation Bible School. Most Daily Vacation Bible Schools enroll a number of people who are not normally a part of the attendance at the normal church functions. After Daily Vacation Bible School has concluded, a careful look through the registration cards of those who have been in attendance, will show a number of families who can be visited by people from the church. A good Daily Vacation Bible School can produce enough prospects to keep a team of callers busy for a quarter of profitable visitation.

DOOR TO DOOR[3]

Another means of acquiring prospects is door to door visitation, sometimes called "cold turkey" calling. This normally is a poor method of finding prospects, and so a church worker should not waste much time on it, but it certainly is better than sitting at home and bemoaning the fact that one has no prospects to call upon.

WEDDINGS AND FUNERALS[4]

A tenth method to find prospects that has proven very beneficial is

---

3. Acts 20:20.
4. Jesus' ministry included attendance at weddings and funerals. He began His ministry at a wedding. He broke up every funeral He attended.

that of weddings and funerals. During pre-marital counseling the author normally asks permission to come into the home to teach the persons about Christ. Many times people have come to Christ or become a part of the church because of the contact that was begun at a wedding. Not only are the bride and groom prospects, but the parents of both bride and groom are also prospects. A call in the home upon one who has been recently married is very productive.

Funerals are wonderful opportunities to minister for Christ. Normally when a husband or wife has died, or a child or parent, grief will persist for a number of months. A person may grieve as long as six months to one year. It is in good taste for the minister or families from the church to call on the bereaved after their loss. This is an excellent opportunity to find people who could be interested in the church. People after a bereavement are excellent prospects and are ready to listen to a message from God.

BUSING

Another suggestion is that of bus routes. Busing can have many hangups, and a church should do ample research before entering this type of program. Many good books have been written by those who have been involved in busing.[5]

Busing can produce excellent prospects. If interested people from a church will choose one particular road out of town and visit each house with an invitation to ride the bus and then run the bus regularly, it has been proven in times past to be a means of producing prospects and converts for the church. The primary object is to get the children into Sunday School. Usually children are more likely to ride the bus than adults. After the children have begun to attend and have a good rapport with the church, it is in proper taste to call on the parents. This produces an opportunity to get into the home and talk to people about Christ.

VAN WATCHING

Another means that has proven effective for many churches is van

---

5. Elmer Towns, *The Successful Sunday School and Teachers Guidebook*, (Carol Stream, Illinois: Creation House, 1976), p. 155-174.

watching. New people move into the community quite regularly. The new people moving into the community are the best prospects for the church. They can readily be seen as an Allied, Mayflower, or U-Haul truck pulls into the community. When the people begin to unload furniture, it is a dead give-away that someone new is moving in. They will be looking for friends, and possibly will be looking for a church home. Usually these folks are most receptive to a friendly visit. It is a good time to take over some goodies and share some refreshments of coffee, tea, or punch and cookies, while they are moving into their home. This provides an excellent opportunity for new people to be won. It is reported that on one street a Christian couple won five families to Christ by watching for new people moving into the community. On another street, in one major community, a family won six other families to Christ because of being van watchers. Remember to be neighborly; don't be pushy, but invite them to church and bring them with you the very first time.

EVERYDAY — EVERYWHERE[6]

Another means of finding prospects is just keeping one's eyes open every day, everywhere one goes. Such places as parent-teacher associations, Boy Scouts, Cub Scouts, at the golf course, the grocery store, and the service station — all are real good places to look for prospects. Insurance men, bankers, and others are good prospects for the gospel of Jesus Christ for one who is always looking for an opportunity to share Jesus with those around him. If a person will look for prospects every day, everywhere he goes, he will come up with several good prospects in the course of a year. You will run across many prospects in the action of every day life.

PUT A VISITOR TO WORK

A fourteenth way to make prospects into members is to put a visitor

---

6. Acts 1:8 ". . . and you shall be my witnesses both in Jerusalem, and in all Judea and Samaria, and even to the remotest part of the earth."

to work. It is reported that the Mormon church has over three thousand jobs for their people. They are masters at giving a new person in the community a job. I believe a person would be spending his time well if he would think of jobs for the new people who come to the church. People will go to a church where they can serve and where they feel needed. People want to be useful. Of course, there are some jobs that non-members cannot do. But there are many other jobs that can be given to people who are not yet members of the church. This will bring them back to the services and make them feel a part and useful in the community.

INSIDE CHURCH CENSUS

More could be said about census. Inside-the-church census is very important and should be used. It is a good practice to list all of those un-saved people within the church who attend regularly. An inside census in one church found a hundred prospects during a revival meeting, forty of whom became Christians before the end of the meeting. People who were in attendance at most of the church services, but were not yet Christians, were found and won to Christ, right within the realm of the church.

In conclusion, it is important to remember that enthusiasm and op-timism are keys to growth within the church. Pessimism is the curse of the church. The leadership of the church should constantly put down negativism. Put negative thoughts out of your mind and the minds of people. Have the attitude of the apostle Paul, "I can do all things through Christ who strengthens me."[7] Remember to continually talk up the good that is happening in the church. Of course, all churches will make mistakes. We should learn from these mistakes, but not dwell on them or publicize them. Learn to expect great things and great things will begin to happen.

Every facet of the church should be undergirded with prayer and a belief that God will hear and answer these prayers. If the church will do all within its power, prospects will literally be found everywhere around the church and in the community. God will bless those that continually seek that which is lost.

---

7. Philippians 4:13.

Chapter 16 Examination

1. What is a common problem with small churches according to our text?

2. How can one take "an in-church survey?"

3. How can one take "a Bible School survey?"

4. How can silent roll call cards produce prospects?

5. Prepare a sample handout brochure for the church you attend.

6. How can we take a religious census?

7. List five other ways to find prospects.

8. What is the value of giving a visitor at church a job?

17

USING A UNIQUE APPROACH TO OPEN A CONVERSATION ABOUT THE GOSPEL OF JESUS CHRIST

". . . I have become all things to all men, that I may by all means save some." I Corinthians 9:22

The apostle Paul spoke of becoming all things to all men, that he might by these means win some to Christ. Certainly we need to be as willing as Paul to adapt to the circumstances in order to open a conversation for Jesus.

While talking in the post office one day to a Baptist minister, the postmaster hollered across the post office and said, "Mr. Crane, you don't talk to Baptist ministers, do you?" I replied, "Why sure I do, Mr. Taylor. I'm a Baptist — in fact, I'm not only a Baptist, I'm a Methodist, an Episcopalian, a Presbyterian, and a real Catholic; in fact, I believe that our church is the real Latter Day Saint Church."

I proceeded to explain, "The New Testament Church believes in baptism by immersion, thus could be called a Baptist church; the New Testament Church believes in following Biblical methods, thus could be called the Methodist Church; the New Testament Church is ruled over by the *presbyteros,* or elders, and thus is a Presbyterian Church. The true church includes all of the saved people who have been saved from the day of Pentecost until the present time. Since the word 'catholic' means 'universal,' only the true church is truly catholic, or universal. The church to which I belong," I continued, "is catholic in that it includes all saved people who have ever lived from the beginning of the church even until the end of time. According to the second chapter of Acts, verse seventeen, we are living in the last days; and according to Romans 1:7, we are called to be saints, thus we are latter day saints." I went on to explain to the people that I, personally, was sick and tired of all the sectarianism and denominationalism in the world and had gone back to simply being a Christian, and thus was not going to be involved in the party spirit that was being displayed by many people in the world today. We simply uphold Christ and His word and seek to be a New Testament church. Thus was afforded the opportunity of witnessing for Christ in a public building, in a post office. There were a number of people who stopped to listen to the conversation before it was finished and it presented a wonderful opportunity to witness for Christ.

On another occasion, I was riding in an elevator. When the elevator operator inquired at which floor I wanted to get off, I asked to go up. When we had reached the top floor, the elevator operator said, "You can't go on up." I replied, "But I want to go on up." She said, "But how can you go up from here?" It was from this point that I introduced the subject of Jesus Christ. I explained that when the time came to be called, I wanted to be prepared to give an account before the great white throne of judgment of Jesus Christ. This presented an opportunity to talk to the lady about Christ.

Often times when asked in a restaurant (particularly in the intermountain area) if I would like a cup of coffee, I reply, "No, thank you, I'm L.D.S." Usually the person will return and say, "What ward do you belong to?" Then I explain that I'm not a Mormon, but am living in the last days and I'm one of the true saints of God. This provides an opportunity to talk to them about Jesus Christ.

On another occasion, when coming to the door of a house, the lady said, "No, thank you, I'm not interested in the church. I'm Jewish." To which the response was, "Oh, that's interesting. I'm half Jewish also, could I come in and talk to you?" The lady asked, "Was it your mother or father?" My reply was, "Neither, it was my older brother. You see, I was adopted into a Jewish family and my older brother, Jesus Christ, is a full-blooded Jew and I am a child of Abraham by faith." This provided the opportunity to explain to the lady how she could become a child of

Abraham in the true sense of the word, by faith, like the faith of Abraham, her father. You see, an opportunity can be made to talk about Jesus Christ if you will only use your imagination and try a unique approach.

Dr. Jack Hyles is a master of making an opportunity to talk to people about Christ. The following article appeared in the *Sword of the Lord*, some years back:

I have always felt that the Lord opens opportunities whereby we can witness easily and appropriately. If we ask the Holy Spirit to guide us, certainly He will open doors and avenues for us to witness. Just a few days ago, I was in a Southern City. I checked into the motel about three in the afternoon. I went to my room, but the room was not clean; the bed was not made. I picked up the telephone, called the office and said to the lady, "I am in my room; I just checked in. The room is a mess! The maid has not cleaned the room; in fact, I'm sure it hasn't been touched since last night."

She said, "That's the only room in the entire place I have available. I guess the maid forgot. I'll send someone right down."

As the maid came in I said, "Well, I'm glad your place is ready, in spite of the fact that mine wasn't." She said, "What?" She was from Europe and had a broken accent.

I said, "I'm glad your place is ready in spite of the fact that mine isn't."

"What do you mean?"

"Your place is ready."

"I haven't received a room anywhere."

"I know it, but it's ready in case you want to reserve it."

"Mister, are you in the motel business?"

"No, but your room is ready in case you want to reserve it. It's all prepared now."

"Where?"

"Heaven." I turned to John 14 where our Lord said, "I go to prepare a place for you. And if I go and prepare a place for you, I will come again, and receive you unto myself, that where I am, there ye may be also."

There in the room, before she ever prepared my place, she accepted and made reservation for her prepared place.

As she was cleaning the room, I went out and took a walk. I got to thinking about all the different ways we can reach people for Christ and all the different times I have seen people saved, because of being appropriate.

Once I spoke to an accountant and said, "Can I help you balance your books?" To a druggist in Garland, Texas, with whom I had traded a long time, I said, "Do you have the Balm of Gilead, here?" He didn't know

191

what the Balm of Gilead was. I told him it was Jesus! Jesus is the precious ointment that can heal. The druggist was saved. To a jeweler in another state, I said, "Do you have the Pearl of great price?"

. . . A young lady was going the wrong way on a one-way street and a fellow said to her, "Hey, lady, you're going the wrong way!" She changed directions and then told him he was going the wrong way and won him to Christ.

In Amarillo, Texas, I was walking down the street one day and saw no one was in a floral shop and so I went in and said to the florist, "Do you have the Rose of Sharon or the Lily of the Valley?" She didn't know what I was talking about, but I got to win her to Christ while I was there.

To a real estate man in Kalamazoo, Michigan, I said, "Can I list a house with you?"

He said, "You certainly may. Where is it?" I said, "In Heaven."

. . . The truth is, there are all kinds of opportunities that God opens for us to win folk to Christ if we would only take those opportunities.[1]

There are many places that a person can witness; for example, buses, planes, and trains present wonderful opportunities to witness for Jesus Christ. Places of business are wonderful opportunities to talk to a person about Jesus, even though time is limited, a gospel tract can be handed out to people. Bus stations, airports, and train terminals are also places where people are idle and one can begin a conversation about Jesus Christ. Such places as washaterias, or parks can be excellent locations to talk about Jesus. Even when one goes to a shopping center, he can begin a conversation and find time to witness for Jesus Christ, if he is "instant in season and out of season."[2]

It has been said that there are eight tips to soul winning that can be used to good advantage. First, one can look for an object to begin a conversation; maybe the object can be a small pup or a child. One could begin talking about the cute little pup, playing around the yard, and then change the conversation to, "Isn't it wonderful that God has made such delightful little creatures to tell us of His love?"

Or a person might ask someone a question. People are usually flattered when a question is asked, and then, after having asked the questions, such as directions, then one could suggest that he would be glad to tell them how to get to heaven.

---

1. Dr. Jack Hyles, *Sword of the Lord Magazine.*
2. Dr. Jack Hyles, *Let's Build an Evangelistic Church,* (Murfreesboro, Tennessee: Sword of the Lord Publishers, 1962) pp. 81-84.

A good deed can be used to begin a conversation about Christ. There are many ways that it can be done, such as helping a widow roof her house. Often times such actions, when done selflessly, will get the attention of neighbors and others and they will be wondering why we are willing to help people. When a person has asked why we are helping another, it gives an opportunity to explain how much Jesus has been willing to help us.

Special events have been used to begin conversation, such as war, famine, or earthquake. When a person comments on these things, the conversation can be quickly and easily turned over to a discussion of Jesus Christ and how He gives us assurance in time of tragedy.

Testimony is another means, especially effective with children. An especially effective testimony was told to the author in Jerusalem by an Arab guide. The Arab guide, while leading us on a tour through the city of Old Jerusalem, asked that we step into an old, street side cafe for a drink. He bought drinks for all of us, and then asked that we sit down. He said he wanted to talk to us for a little while. He explained that during the process of the Six Day War, he had been separated from his wife and two boys. They had been visiting in Damascus when the war broke out. For a period of many months he heard not a word from his boys or his wife. He said that three or four times a day he went to the mosque to beseech Allah on behalf of his children, without so much as a sound or word from them.

One day when things were going so poorly that he could hardly carry on, a minister spoke to him and asked why the guide was so despondent. He took the opportunity to explain to the minister about his despondency and the minister then asked him why he didn't go home that evening and pray to Jehovah God, through the name of Jesus Christ, for the safe return of his wife and children.

He went on to tell us that it was the very next morning that a letter came postmarked from the Red Cross, telling about the safety of his wife and children. In less than a week they were reunited. He bore the personal testimony to us that Jesus is the access to God, the Father, and prayers addressed through Jesus Christ bring answers. He said he hoped that all of us were Christians. He used his personal testimony in a dramatic way to tell us about Jesus and what He meant to him. He explained that because of answered prayer he had become a Christian and was a faithful Christian to that day.

Songs can be used to bear a testimony to those around us. A song that is whistled or sung, happily, while about one's work, will bear a testimony to those who hear it. They will be hearing, but probably not objecting to the testimony that is born through song. The message will get across to them.

Sometimes a fact can be used to begin a conversation; for example, one might begin with the facts of Masada, the place where the Jewish zealots held out against the Roman army for three and a half years.[3] It is an easy matter to turn the conversation from the mass suicide of the 960 Jewish people on top of Fort Masada to a conversation about the prophecy made in Matthew 24, when Jesus the Lord predicted that there would be a time of trouble come upon the Jewish people because of their rejection of Him. This time of trouble, He said, would be worse than anything that had happened at any time in the past or future history of the world.

Other facts, such as the resurrection, or fulfilled prophecy, can be used as a springboard to get a conversation going about Jesus Christ.

A final means that can be used to start a conversation about Christ is prayer. Whether a person be sick or one is just wanting to talk to him about Christ, prayer can be a springboard to get him thinking about his relationship to God. One time two preachers, after trying to talk to a man about Christ on many different occasions, finally asked if it would be all right for them to pray with him. He said it would be okay, and so one preacher said, "Why don't you pray? Won't you repeat these words after me?" The man agreed that he would repeat the words after him. And so the preacher framed these words, "Dear God," and the man repeated, "Dear God." Then the preacher said, "Goodbye." And the man repeated, "Goodbye, " after him. The preacher then said, "I'm going to hell." At the close of this brief prayer, the man was in tears and it was only a matter of hours until he made the decision to become a Christian. I'm not suggesting such a blunt prayer be used, but prayer can be used as a means of starting a conversation to talk about Jesus Christ.

Inconvenience can be used to good advantage to open a conversation about Christ. Last March the author was in Southern Egypt at a lit-

---

3. Yigael Yadan, *Masada*, (3032 Grays Inn Road, London: Sphere Books, Limited).

tle outpost of civilization. When checking to confirm return flight reservations, it was found that no reservations had been made by the travel agent. There were no spaces on the plane for nine days and no room in the only hotel. It was a classic time for anger. Instead it became an opportunity for Christ.

A well-dressed gentleman was engaged in conversation. He was a general in the Egyptian army. He said he was Islamic. He asked what my work was. It provided a wonderful opportunity to talk to him about Christ. The conversation was most positive and he listened intently.

Shortly after arriving home, a letter arrived from him. His words were, "Now that I have become a believer what should I do? Can you send me instructions and a Bible?" It was a new case of an officer of the king coming to Christ. Our inconvenience was his opportunity to know Christ.

The apostle seems to be using this method in introducing his preaching in Athens. He begins with information very familiar to them and moves from that to things unfamiliar. He began by finding them where they were.

> And Paul stood in the midst of the Areopagus and said, "Men of Athens, I observe that you are very religious in all respects. For while I was passing through and examining the objects of your worship, I also found an altar with the inscription, TO AN UNKNOWN GOD. What therefore you worship in ignorance, this I proclaim to you" Acts 17:22-23.

Paul's message to the Athenians produced favorable results. Dionysius the Areopagite and Damaris believed. His willingness to use a unique approach opened the way for his message.

Using a unique approach can be a powerful means to get people to start thinking about their relationship to Jesus Christ, the Savior. No approach will get much done without persistent, penitential prayer.

Chapter 17 Examination

1. List several ways one can open a conversation with someone about Christ.

2. What sorts of places can we witness for Christ? List ten or more. Show how.

3. List eight tips to soul winning as given in the text.

4. How can prayer be used to open a conversation about Christ?

5. Give an illustration of how inconvenience can be used to talk about Christ.

6. All approaches to people about Christ must be accompanied with
_____.

18

ORGANIZING SHEPHERDING

"Therefore, I exhort the elders among you, as your fellow elder and witness of the sufferings of Christ, and a partaker also of the glory that is to be revealed, Shepherd the flock of God among you, not under compulsion, but voluntarily, according to the will of God: and not for sordid gain, but with eagerness. . . ." I Peter 5:1-2

One of the problems that plague the average preacher is that he is so busy shepherding and pastoring the saved, that he has little time to be involved in the work of reaching those who are lost. By the time he calls upon all the people that are sick, shut-in, and suffering from various kinds of personal or emotional problems, his time is so consumed that he has had little time to reach out to those who are lost.

The scripture's teaching is clear that the elders or bishops within the church are to be shepherds of the flock and are to oversee the spiritual welfare of the people. In reality this often does not happen. It may not be that the elders or bishops are unwilling, they just do not know how to go about their work. They have never had their work organized in such a way as to make it obtainable for them. The following suggestions are offered in the hope that it will make it much easier for the evangelist or preacher to be involved, along with many other people in the church, in the work of reaching the lost for Jesus Christ.

A careful study of I Timothy 3:1-7 and Titus 5:1-9, as compared with Acts 20:17-32 and I Peter 5:1-5, shows that the elders, bishops, or overseers have the job of taking care of the flock of God. These passages teach that elders are to have the responsibility of looking after the sheep. They can and should free the hands of others within the body for the work of reaching out to the lost. The church today needs to mobilize the elders.

A successful church will involve the membership in the work. Shepherding is a very important way that the membership can be involved. The elders must work to see that each person grows satisfactorily in Christ and see that those who stray from the fold are brought back into the fellowship with Christ and His church. God's plan is a beautiful one. It brings involvement, strength, vitality and health to the church.

How can shepherding, then, be organized within the church? The first step is to prepare a membership directory that is available to each elder, possibly each member, that lists every person who is a part of the fellowship of the local church. It is hard to shepherd a group of people when one does not know who they are.

After the membership directory has been made, it would be well to find one elder who is especially interested in the backslidden or in the membership of the church. Place him as head over the shepherding program. Working with this man, it is possible to divide up the membership into six, eight, ten, or twenty groups, depending upon how many elders and how many members the church may have. Each elder can be responsible for ten to fifteen families that are backslidden or not faithful. It is then the responsibility of that elder over a period of three months to either visit these people, or see that someone else visits them. The caller should find out why they have not been properly functioning within the church.

The membership directories can be color-coded so that each elder's charge or responsibility is marked in a different color of ink to indicate the ones for which they are responsible. After a three month period, the groups can be alternated to different elders. One elder may not have as much influence on one person as another. While one elder may be offensive, the other elder may be exactly what the person needs in order to be restored to the church.

A great deal can be accomplished over the course of one year when four different elders call in the homes of the backslidden or indifferent church members. Each in turn can talk with them about their responsibility to Christ and His church.

This is not as heavy a burden as it at first would seem. Ten people, visited over a three month period, would only amount to a couple of calls a week on the part of each elder. This is simply fulfilling his normal duty as a part of God's family.

Some elder may be balky and not willing to work with the suggested program. This elder might be given the assistance of a dedicated deacon who likes to call. He can be the overseer, while the deacon actually does the calling. When he sees the progress that is being made in the church because of the work of the elders, he will eventually get excited about the program and become directly involved himself. The end result of all this is that shepherding frees the evangelist, preacher, and evangelistic calling team to do their work of reaching out to those who are lost.

When a new family comes into the church, they should be assigned a family to oversee them for a period of six or eight weeks. The minute they respond to the invitation and are baptized, or transfer their membership to the local church, a family with similar interests and of similar age should be assigned to help them in the early weeks of becoming a part of the church. This family can sit with them and introduce them to their Sunday School classes. If they do not show up for one of the church services, it is the sponsoring family's responsibility to call on them in their home.

It is also the responsibility of the shepherding family to invite them to their home or to a restaurant for dinner during this initial six or eight week period.[1] Thus, the new family is warmly introduced into the life of the church. After eight weeks of caring for them, it will not be easy for the sponsoring family to forget them in the months to come. The new family will also be introduced to the work of the church. Shepherding can be a means of really vitalizing the life of the church.

After shepherding had been introduced into a church of about 250 in attendance, by actual count, forty people were restored to the church services in just one week. The elders had been out shepherding those who were backslidden. Shepherding is one key to being a BOLD ONE FOR CHRIST and getting the church really involved in its real ministry.

Shepherds will certainly want to pray continually for their flock and

---

1. Hospitality is one of the qualifications for a church leader. I Timothy 3:2; Titus 1:8.

for the lost. Have you prayed for the lost today? Right now is a good time.

Chapter 18 Examination

1. What common problem plagues most preachers hindering them from being an evangelist and equipper?

2. What is a chief duty of the church elders? Give Scriptures as proof.

3. The first step in organizing shepherding in the church is to prepare a

_____ .

4. How can you find someone to oversee the shepherding, who should be put in charge?

5. How should the minister react to an elder, who is balky and not wanting to be a shepherd?

6. When a new member comes into the church, they should be assigned a sponsoring family or shepherd. What things should be done with them the first six weeks they are members, according to the text?

7. Shepherding must be undergirded with _____.

8. What will shepherding do for many churches?

19

HOSPITAL AND NURSING HOME VISITATION

". . . I was a stranger, and you invited me in: naked, and you clothed me: I was sick, and you visited me: I was in prison, and you came to me . . . truly I say to you, to the extent that you did it to one of the brothers of mine, even the least of them you did to me." Matthew 25:37 & 40

In order for one to properly minister to people in the hospital, it is necessary that we understand how complex hospital care is today. When we consider the many types of treatment offered in the average hospital, along with the complex biological nature of our human bodies it certainly is a sobering thing to enter into this process as a witness on behalf of Jesus Christ. In spite of their complex nature our bodies are not just machines that need repair, but they are also spirit and emotion.

Today's health care is looking more and more towards the spiritual and emotional aspects of man's being, as well as his physical. One psychologist from a major hospital in New York City made the statement that nearly every physical ailment begins in the mind of man. As many as sixty-five percent of all people hospitalized are hospitalized because of spiritual and emotional problems which have led to physical ailments.

Whether one agrees with these statistics or not, it will be well to recognize the inter-dependence of mind and body. The healing effect of peace of mind upon the sick person is quite important. A Decatur, Illinois hospital ran a test for a period of one year in which they tried to judge the difference between people who had faith in God and those who did not. Those with faith recovered one-third more quickly than those without. Therefore, it is imperative that we Christians find a place in the hospital to minister on behalf of Jesus Christ.

Just what can be done with integrity in the hospital for our Lord? First of all, the hospital is a good place for pre-evangelism. Hospital visitation can be a place where friends are made. A short, friendly, cheerful visit in the hospital room, possibly even a brief prayer if the patient so desires, will build friendship for the church. Many times a call at the hospital on a backslidden church member will mark the beginning of his return to the fold. Calling on the sick in the hospital shows one's concern for them.

There are a number of rules that should be observed in hospital visitation. We might say that there are ten commandments that will help one to be most effective in hospital visitation.

1. VISIT EARLY

Visit early, before a crowd of relatives and friends arrive. Most hospitals have become aware of the value of visitors from the church, primarily a preacher, or elder, and have made it possible for church workers of this nature to visit at times other than regular visiting hours. It is wise to visit at times when there is not a crowd of people in the hospital room.

2. BE BRIEF

People who are ill do not need someone leaning over their bed and preaching to them. A short visit of five minutes can be much more valuable than one of fifteen or twenty minutes that leaves them uneasy and imposes upon them while they are ill.

3. USE LITERATURE

People have time to read while in the hospital. *A Living New Testa-*

ment, *Good News for Modern Man,* a little church paper, or devotional book is often really appreciated by the person and will get him thinking about his spiritual life.

4. BE FRIENDLY

Be friendly to those you are visiting and those in other beds. If there is another person in the room, it is appropriate to include him in your conversation and when you pray for the sick person.

5. ALWAYS SEE PEOPLE BEFORE MAJOR SURGERY

People, even though familiar with the hospital routine, will be very anxious before major surgery. A prayer at that time will be really appreciated, long remembered, and will build good will towards Christ and the church.

6. PRAY WITH SICK PEOPLE

If the person is a member of the church, already a Christian, it is unnecessary to ask him if he would like prayer. If not, it is only polite to ask before praying with someone who is ill.

7. LET THEM TALK

Be sure to let them talk about their condition. Don't just come right out and ask them what is wrong. Encourage them and ask them how they are feeling, and what sort of attitude they have towards their hospitalization. If they want to talk, listen to them. Be very careful to listen to what they have to say. Our world is in much need of people who care enough to listen.

8. SPEAK WELL OF THE CHURCH

Put in a good word for the church. It does not need to be a lengthy sermon or dissertation on the church. Let them know that you are there on behalf of the church and Jesus Christ.

9. TEACH GENTLY

Be ready to teach them if they are open to the idea. The hospital room is not a place to twist arms and coerce people to listen to you talk about the church or about Christ. A person strapped to a bed, confined to a room, may ill appreciate an aggressive preacher or church person, coming in to cram religion down their throat. It may simply make them more ill and be a very inconsiderate and un-Christian thing for one to do.

10. OBSERVE THE RULES OF THE HOSPITAL

Do not violate the rules of the hospital or you will find yourself being asked to leave and not return. These ten rules will help you in basic hospital ministry.

It can be of advantage to send get-well cards to those who are in the hospital. A sunshine committee may be several older ladies in the church who can be called each week with a list of those who are ill. They can send cards on behalf of the church. It will build good will.

Do not use the hospital as a place to proselyte people from other churches. This breeds bad will and brings additional tension upon a person while they are ill. It heightens their worry and increases the problem of stress. One time the author walked into a room and found the curtain drawn around the bed of the patient he had come to see. He listened intently for a moment to see if the doctor was with the patient, fulfilling some hospital routine. It became apparent that a preacher from another church was heavily proselyting this member of the author's church. The author stepped around the curtain and said, "Oh, excuse me, I didn't realize she was a member of your church." The lady, with a perplexed look on her face, said, "Oh, I'm not a member of his church, I'm a member of your church." To which the author replied, "I thought that was the case, but I was confused for a moment." A proselyter was put in his proper place. Again, remember not to use the hospital as a place to proselyte people for your church. If they already have a church of their own and you want to talk to them, wait until they are home.

The dynamics of the hospital room should be understood by one who is going to visit in the hospital. The first thought that comes to the mind of the person who is admitted to the hospital is the fear of death. Even though the person may not have anything very seriously wrong with him, he still will not understand all of the hospital routines. Many fears may be lurking in the back of his mind. Even though he puts on a smiling facade his thought may be, "I may die."

It is reported that a preacher went in to visit a lady he did not know at all. After sitting down beside her bed, without introducing himself, he said, "Are you going to die?" The lady's response was, "I hope not, thank you. Who are you and would you please leave?" The lady had been having problems that she, herself, had pre-diagnosed as cancer and was afraid of death. Such an unkind approach by the minister had added to her fear.

Another tension of the hospital room is fear of pain. People don't like to hurt and yet many hospital routines hurt; shots, blood transfusions, and blood samples being drawn. All of this adds to the fear of pain. Lurking even in the back of a somewhat healthy person's mind will be this fear.

A third dynamic of a hospital room is that of uncertainty. "What is going to happen to me next?" Strange medical procedures, strange food, strange clothes, all help to make the person uncertain and lead to tensions while in the hospital. While there, modesty will be violated by diabolical gowns that leave a person's rear side exposed; nurses, doctors and technicians coming in to prod and examine; one who has a sense of modesty will really feel uneasy. Add to this strange foods, strange beds, equipment, financial woes, and expense — worry will be the result. Insert along with this a gruff doctor or head nurse, who may be having a hard time coping with the person's illness and is trying to cover up his own uncertainty with a gruff approach, and the result is a patient in quiet panic.

How can we, as concerned Christians, help to desensitize tensions? First, we must cope with our own tensions about death. If we enter the room and are afraid of the strange things that are going on there, we may communicate through our face or the tone of our voice, our own fears. We must cope with our own feelings before entering the room.

We should go there to bring some peace and faith to the hospital scene, out of love of Jesus Christ and the person being visited.

Enter the room with warmth and kindness; speak in a soft, but audible calm voice. Be aware of the body language of the person. Use the gestalt principle of reading the eyes, the face, and the hands to pick up tensions. Respond to the fear that may be expressed or observed in the patient.

Be a good listener. Sometimes it seems the whole world is looking for someone who has time to listen. Yes, we may be busy, but time spent letting a person ventilate their fears, frustrations and concerns may be well spent time in pre-evangelism.

Touch, also is valuable, unless the person has some highly contagious communicable disease. It would be wise for a young man to be careful how he touches a young woman who is not his wife or a relative. But touch can be a valuable way of communicating concern between men, or between a man and an older woman.

Of course, prayer is a natural and wonderful means of desensitizing tension. If the prayer can be expressed in a normal and comforting way, it will be a great help to the person.

The presence of a kind person in the hospital room, who is greatly concerned about the condition of the patient, will be a great asset in pre-evangelism and may pave the way for that person to come to Christ.

How will a patient respond to these tensions? In Dr. Elisabeth Kubler-Ross's classic book, *On Death and Dying*,[1] five stages of grief are listed. These stages can be observed in the life of a person who is suffering from a chronic illness or one who is only going through very serious surgery.

The first stage of grief is that of denial. Denial is a buffer, sort of a spiritual shock absorber. Sometimes we would call it unbelief. The person refuses to accept the fact that he is critically and terminally ill. Both the patient and his family will experience this time of denial after first learning of the seriousness of the illness. A person needs to be kindly brought to the place where he can accept the truth. Our awareness that they will go through a period of not accepting the seriousness of their illness can be a real asset in dealing with them.

---

1. Elisabeth Kubler-Ross, *On Death and Dying*, (New York: The Macmillan Company, 1969), pp. 36-44.

The second stage that we can observe in the seriously, or chronically, ill person is that of anger. Even though to a Christian it would seem a lack of faith, often times a person, even one with faith, will yell at the family and ask why God has let this serious illness come upon them. The person may bite at the nurses and be resentful. Really their resentment is not towards the family member, minister, or the church member. The resentment is anger because of the futility of the situation in which they find themselves. All they can do is respond by getting angry. At this point, the Christian worker needs to be very careful to respond lovingly and understand that the anger is not directed at them or God, but at the situation.

A third reaction that we need to recognize is that of bargaining. The critically, chronically ill person will try to make bargains with God. They may make outlandish promises. They might turn to faith healers or to strange treatments. This is an effort to seek help beyond the normal means of hospital, doctor, and prayer. Desperately, they are seeking for an extension of their lives. They may demand special care from the nurses, or want the doctor to be extra nice to them. They may also be extra nice to the doctor in the hopes that they will get better care and as a result be the rare person who will beat this illness.

At a time like this, we can help the person draw on his resource of faith. God often does hear and answer the prayer for the sick and it certainly is a means of strength for them.

When none of these coping methods seem to work, depression will often set in. When denial is no longer possible, and they recognize that their body is in a state of terminal illness or will be permanently marred, whether it be with a colostomy, mastectomy, or other type of treatment, they then will plunge into a deep depression. This is the beginning of acceptance. They are accepting the fact that there will be many unrealized goals and dreams. At this point cold fear can set in. Now is the time when the Christian worker can be a great asset as he goes to help the person realize that all is not lost. Just because a person has suffered some type of marring of the body or some type of terminal illness, it still is not the end. As Christians, we can live victoriously through the remaining time we have and can trust God. God has prepared a beautiful new world where we will never suffer an impairment of the body in any way. The depressed person can really be helped by the Christian worker.

209

Then, of course, there is the matter of acceptance. The last stage of grief is that of acceptance. It is easier for the Christian person to come to a stage of acceptance than the non-Christian, because of his understanding of life after death. The object of the Christian worker is to work through the first four stages of grief so that the time a person has left can be used beneficially and as enjoyably as possible. They may use it to be with their families or to take a trip or to accomplish some last project that they are interested in. If the person is not terminal, only going to have an impairment of their body, they need to accept this fact and do what they can to enjoy life in spite of the fact that some avenue of enjoyment might be cut off for them. *The Healing of Our Grief*,[2] by Dr. Bruce Parmenter, and *Good Grief*,[3] by Granger Westberg, would be very helpful reading in this area of ministry.

Remember that the non-terminal patient can also experience these stages of grief in a lesser or greater degree. Watch for them.

When dealing with the hospital or nursing home patient, remember that pre-evangelism is simply going and making contact, making yourself available to talk to people about their needs. It is not a time to push church or Christ upon the person. However, when a person is terminal, modification of this principle is in order. Be really ready to talk to them when the opportunity presents itself. If a person is terminal, it might be a wonderful opportunity to suggest that you would like to visit with them, when they get to feeling just a little bit better, about their relationship with Christ.

Nothing can beat genuine love and concern. Be observant of body language, be a good listener. Real concern and love of the patient can be developed as one overcomes his own fear of the hospital. If a person can view his work as a ministry on behalf of the creator Jesus Christ, his hospital ministry will take on deep meaning. Certainly the hospital is an area that should not be neglected by the church, as it is a wonderful place to point people to Christ.

A further note about this area of hospital ministry is needed. Scripture reading can be greatly useful. But be careful to read proper scriptures when talking to the hospital patient. Sometimes certain passages

---

2. Bruce Parmenter, *The Healing of our Grief*, (Lincoln, Illinois: Bruce Parmenter, Publisher, 1974).

3. Granger Westberg, *Good Grief*, (Philadelphia: Fortress Press, 1962).

can do more harm than good. Some suggested passages that are always beneficial are Psalms 23; Psalms 121; John 14:1-3; Romans 8:26-39; and Hebrews 11. Make scripture readings brief and positive. Do not preach. Read in a pleasant, quiet voice.

Hospital ministry is usually a highly neglected field of endeavor for most churches. Is this the area of ministry Christ is pointing you toward? Be regular. Expect to grow and constantly become more effective.

Prayer is a must if the lost are to be reached. Let's pray for the lost and for revival to come to our world.

Chapter 19 Examination

True or False

_____ 1. Hospital ministry is quite simple.

_____ 2. Today's health care is more and more turning away from spiritual and physical care combined.

_____ 3. Ninety-five percent of all people hospitalized are hospitalized because of emotional or spiritual problems according to our text.

_____ 4. The hospital is a good place for indepth evangelism and teaching.

_____ 5. Good ideas to help your hospital calling are:

_____a) Visit early

_____b) Stay 20 minutes or more.

_____c) Use literature

_____d) Be friendly

_____e) Do not visit before major surgery

_____f) Pray with sick people

_____g) Be a good listener

_____h) Criticize the preacher and church

_____i) Do your own thing in spite of hospital rules

_____ 6. The hospital is a good place to proselyte.

_____ 7. The hospital room is full of tensions, real and imagined.

_____ 8. Strange smells, pain, expense, death, flowers, all help the hospital be a tension-filled place.

_____ 9. Speak loud and clear in the hospital room.

_____10. The more theological words you can use, the better in teaching.

_____11. Nothing can beat genuine love and concern in the hospital room.

_____12. Ask a non-church member if they would like you to pray with them before you pray.

20

WIN THE BIG BATTLES

"And this is eternal life, that they may know thee the only true God, and Jesus Christ whom thou hast sent." John 17:3

It is not suggested that personal evangelism should be a battle or a fight, under any circumstances. Usually those who scrap reduce things to scraps. We ought to be very careful to be very kind and considerate with people. At the same time, we ought to realize that we are in a spiritual warfare on behalf of Jesus Christ and are in conflict against the kingdom of Satan. We ought to know where we are going, plan a strategy, hold to that plan and not get side-tracked to other things. Satan is a master of side-tracking and will supply the person you are teaching with a list of things that will keep him from facing the real issue at hand. The following suggestions should be useful.

Don't get side-tracked with questions such as, "Can I smoke if I become a Christian?" or "Can I drink?" or "Is it all right if I'm a social drinker after I become a Christian?" or "What do you think about the Mormons or the Jehovah's Witnesses?" or "How does your church feel about the Catholics?" These questions are simply an effort to divert you from the area where they have the real need and where they feel most sensitive. Satan will keep the person well supplied with questions that are diversionary in nature. Do not be abrupt with the person, but stick with the teaching plan. For example, if you are using the Roman Road to Salvation, courteously keep them on the issue. You might respond by saying, "That is an interesting question, and we need to talk about that, but let's carry this to conclusion, first, and we'll consider that question later." Remember always to be friendly and patient. Abruptness and sarcasm seldom pay off. If a person finds himself getting a little hot under the collar, then pray for patience from God. One of the fruits of the Spirit is that of being long-suffering and it will pay off big dividends in talking with people who do not know Jesus Christ.

People who come to Jesus Christ usually have been brought by one whom they consider a good friend. You need to develop a good relationship with the person with whom you are working. This may take a number of weeks, or months, but it is worth it when we consider that the saving of that soul will change the person's whole eternity. Soul winning is a greater work than building a great skyscraper, bridge, or ship.

A list of do's in giving your personal testimony:

1. Be known in your business and social life for honesty, integrity, and paying your bills promptly.

2. Lead a moral life from an earthly standpoint. Have no unconfessed sins in your life; they will rob you of your power.

3. Realize your testimony is precious in the sight of God and that you are His workman.

4. Desire in your heart to be used of God.

5. Expect God to use you.

6. Speak to God first, that He may speak through you.

7. Study your Bible daily to know why you should testify.

8. Study your Bible daily to know how to testify (Acts 26, for example). Testimony should consist of introduction, before, during, after, and the challenge.

9. Study your Bible daily to know how to use God's word, the Bible, most effectively.

10. Write out your testimony so it will be organized for effectiveness; the ineffectual must and will be eliminated so there will be better communication.

11. Practice giving your testimony privately in order to gain confidence.

12. Be careful of your personal habits, dress, body, and breath.

13. In your presentation, depend upon the power of God, not on your wisdom, wit, or winsomeness.

14. Present a person, Jesus Christ. Keep Jesus Christ central to what you are doing.

15. Let Christ's love shine through you. Be sure to give God's plan of salvation using scriptural references, such as the Roman Road.

16. Stick to the main issue of Christ and salvation.

17. Stay within your time limit.

18. Be sincere.

19. Be truthful.

20. Be tactful.

21. Be enthusiastic.

22. Be positive.

23. Be gentle.

24. Be convincing.

25. Be confident that He will give the victory and realize that the battle is the Lord's not yours.

Here is a list of don'ts:

1. Do not preach.

2. Do not attack a political party, sect, or denomination.

3. Do not ignore the rules.

4. Do not be excessively humorous.

5. Do not talk about God and the Lord, and yet not use the name of Jesus Christ.

6. Do not be vague in relating the events of salvation.

7. Do not detail gory sins.

8. Do not embarass someone in the room. For example, "Sam here, my partner, hasn't been saved."

9. Do not ignore the person being taught, stare over his head, or look in the opposite direction.

10. Do not use ecclesiastical words without definition; for example, "saved," "sanctified," "justified," "washed," "propitiation," and so forth.

11. Do not speak in a monotone.

12. Do not speak in a voice so low that those in far corners cannot hear you.

13. Do not play up the type of work you pursue.

14. Do not frequently interject, "Praise the Lord!"

15. Do not go in dirty clothes, needing a bath, or needing to comb your hair or polish your shoes.

16. Do not go into the home if the people are obviously preoccupied, or have a house full of company.

17. Do not have a poor opening; people will either lose interest or be interested, depending upon your opening.

18. Do not carry unwieldy notes; use a small pocket Bible.

19. Do not use inappropriately funny jokes.

20. Do not close the teaching session with, "Well, my time is up, so I will quit now."

21. Do not give your testimony in your own strength, but in the power of God.

22. Do not tell people that theirs is a ridiculous idea when they interject an idea of what is being taught.

Use these common sense rules, always keeping your eye fixed on the goal of leading the person to know Jesus Christ. When he has come to know Jesus Christ as Lord and master of his life, then he will be able to grow and overcome many of the problems of sin that he has been experiencing. Trying to solve the sin problem in the person's life, without him first knowing Jesus Christ as Lord, is like trying to treat cancer with salve. We want to deal with the issues at hand, kindly and lovingly. Lead the person to know Jesus Christ and help him make Jesus Lord of his life; then a multitude of other problems will be resolved. Remember to fight the big battles and win them. If you persist in being side-tracked and arguing over little issues that come up, you will win many of the little battles, but will lose the war, and the person's soul will be lost eternally. Have you prayed for souls today?

Chapter 20 Examination

True and False

_____ 1. Personal evangelism can often be a real battle.

_____ 2. Don't get sidetracked on such issues as tobacco and alcohol with a non-Christian.

_____ 3. The big issue is, will they let Jesus be Lord of their lives.

_____ 4. Friendship is relatively unimportant in leading a person to Christ.

_____ 5. Your own personal life can lend power to your personal testimony.

_____ 6. Wit, wisdom and learning are quite necessary in soul winning.

_____ 7. Long calls are better than short ones.

_____ 8. Learn to preach to your prospects.

_____ 9. Look at and make eye contact with the person you are teaching.

_____10. The more theological words you can use the better in teaching.

_____11. Be sure to correct every wrong detail the prospect brings up so no false impressions will be left.

_____12. Be careful to win all battles.

21

ORGANIZING BOLD ONES IN THE LOCAL CHURCH

". . . and pray on my behalf, that utterance may be given to me in the opening of my mouth, to make known with boldness the mystery of the gospel . . ." Ephesians 6:19

Most churches lack a plan for action for their calling program. A planned calling program does not mean that the rest of the church should not be involved in daily taking the message of Christ everywhere they are, on their job, etc. It simply means that in addition to all of the other things that are happening, there needs to be a time set aside, when in an organized way, training can be given and calling can be done.

A space of time, from five to ten weeks, preferably ten weeks, should be set aside in which persons will commit themselves to being present each week unless they are hindered by illness or work. These people are not asked individually to participate, but must volunteer, in order to be a part of the program. (A sort of reverse psychology can be used. This is an elite group of volunteers.) Once they have volunteered, they have committed themselves to ten weeks of instruction and ten weeks of calling.

A meal can be served at 6:30 P.M. This need not be a big ordeal for any person. Kentucky Fried Chicken can be picked up and fed the callers. Many other types of ready prepared food are available. Drinks can be provided by the church. While the people are eating their meal, an informal lecture can be given to them for their training. It is suggested that chapters 1, 2, 3, 5, 6, 7, 8, 10, 11, and 12 be used for lectures. The principle that is to be adopted is that of discipleship. The leader will try to call with each BOLD ONE. In this way, teaching and on the job training can be given.

During the training, some role play can be used to demonstrate how to teach. Questions can be answered about various problems that arise while calling. The discipleship principle means that a more experienced caller be assigned to go with one who is new, sharing with them the things that they have learned from past experience.

During the second year of such a program, those who have graduated from the previous year of training are naturals to assign as personal disciplers to help train those who are new in the work of personal evangelism.

After about one hour of training, the group then should be paired up and given cards of prospects to call upon. The group should meet back at the church at about 9:00 P.M. to share the experiences of what has taken place during their calls. Seldom will every group of callers have good calls, but usually there will be several who have. Some decisions for Christ may have been secured. This will be exciting and helpful to the group as a whole.

After each person has shared his own personal experiences of the evening, a circle of prayer can be held which will bring great closeness and a sense of satisfaction to those who have been calling.

One should not expect to immediately become a great caller. It takes years of time for a person to develop fully. If a person will make a commitment and spend week after week out seeking that which is lost, they will find that they will grow and become more and more proficient and have more and more fruit for their labor. We must prepare people to be about the Father's business. A practical calling program such as this can be of great benefit.

After the people have finished the course, it is a good idea to present to them, during the morning church service, a certificate of graduation. They should be publicly congratulated on having become a BOLD ONE for Christ.

Provide the BOLD ONES with calling cards. These calling cards are left on the doors of houses where people have not been home. They can be given to people during the week, with an invitation to come to church.

Brochures can be provided for the callers to leave with people wherever they go. It has been the author's experience that the BOLD ONES will get involved far beyond the Tuesday night calling time after they have had the opportunity to learn and receive confidence in what they are doing.

This can become the basis of a discipling program in the local church. The only way we will ever get the job of evangelizing done is by using the plan Jesus used, discipling. Robert E. Coleman says there are eight steps that Jesus used as His ". . . *Master Plan of Evangelism.*"[1]

These eight steps are: (1) selection, (2) association, (3) consecration, (4) impartation, (5) demonstration, (6) delegation, (7) supervision, and (8) reproduction. Certainly he has really gotten to the heart of the issue. It is very important that you read this fine book. It is simple and to the point.

The BOLD ONES program can become the beginning of big things in the life of the church. One church began with ten persons being trained in discipleship five years ago. This year, they will lead over seven hundred people into the body and sixty-five percent of those will be by baptism. This year they have seventy-five disciplers and seventy-five disciples. Each disciple is given training and then shown how by his leader. It is the principle used by Jesus, and that will make it possible to win our communities to Jesus now.

Such books as *Disciples are Made — Not Born*[2] are indispensable to the person who wants an evangelistic church. God has seldom used those who are unwilling to prepare and work hard for Him. Remember not much happens until we have first prayed.

We need not have small, dead, or dying churches today. Organize BOLD ONES in the church following the suggested format. It will change the church.

---

1. Robert E. Coleman, *The Master Plan of Evangelism*, (Old Tappan, New Jersey: Fleming H. Revell Co., 1963).

2. Walter A. Henrichsen, *Disciples are Made — Not Born.*

Chapter 21 Examination

1. Outline a simple planned calling program for your church, showing a knowledge of the text material.

2. How should callers be teamed up?

3. After organized church calling each evening, how should the evening be concluded?

4. List Coleman's eight steps of Jesus' master plan of evangelism.

5. What Scripture passage does the title, "Bold Ones For Christ" come from? Memorize this verse of Scripture.

6. Two things are necessary if you want to be used by Christ, according to our text. What are they?

22

SOUL WINNING AS A CURE-ALL
FOR THE CHURCH

"The Lord is not slow about his promise, as some count slowness, but is patient toward you, not wishing for any to perish but for all to come repentance." II Peter 3:9

There is not any one program that will cure all the ills in the church, but there are few programs that will do more to bring health and vitality to a church than for that church to become really involved in evangelism. There are few things that will bring more joy to the fellowship of the church than to see people baptized into Christ weekly. When Christians see people coming to make the good confession, tears will come to their eyes. When people's lives are completely changed from ruin and despair to usefulness and success in the work of the church, enthusiasm will mount.

Soul winning has proven to be a cure for financial woes. A church that has a lagging membership will usually be suffering financial woes, but when people come into the church it will be a new source of income. A church or a business that does not have enough income needs more customers, more people. As new people come into the church, the budget of the church will begin to expand and as the older members see that the church is really reaching the lost for Christ, they will dig deeper in their pockets. It has been demonstrated time and again that the financial needs of the church will be met if the church is evangelistic.

The second thing that is cured by personal evangelism is that of lagging membership. The membership becomes discouraged when they go Sunday after Sunday without seeing anyone become a Christian. However, when the word gets around that week after week, people are walking the aisle to make the good confession and to be buried in Christian baptism, the membership that has been disinterested will begin to show an interest in things that are going on at the church. The church will begin to grow; attendance will set new records and, in general, the church will get all excited about what is going on.

The "musical chairs" of the ministry is cured by soul winning. Many ministers leave churches because of a sense of failure; or because of a lack of enthusiasm or interest in what they are doing, the church fires them. It all goes back to a church not producing new membership. Certainly it is not the minister's total responsibility, as we have outlined throughout this book, but when the church does not grow, he will get the blame. He is to be the leader or the spark plug to help the people become equipped to do this work. When a church is growing and membership continues to increase, week after week, year after year, that church would be very foolish to ask for the resignation of their preacher.

Soul winning cures the "need for workers" syndrome in the church. Many churches do not have enough teachers to teach Sunday School, enough workers to work in the Junior Church department, or in the youth work of the church. When new members begin to become a part of the church, these people will want and need to be involved. These people will sing in the choir, sing special music, will be willing to serve in all of the different capacities in which the church serves the community. As the modern day church becomes thoroughly evangelistic like the early church, it will be back to the successes of the early church. The church can and will make a change in the whole community. Not only will the church be changed, but the church's influence will be felt all over town. As people from all walks of life are changed, and their lives are made vital for Christ, the church will be central in the life of the town. So not only is soul winning a cure-all for the church, but it is a cure-all for the community. It will make it a better place in which to live. Soul winning is the number one business of the church and prayer is the key. Let's be about the Master's business.

Chapter 22 Examination

1. What program will solve *all* church ills?

2. How can soul winning help the church financially?

3. How can soul winning help solve the "musical chairs" of the ministry?

4. Soul winning can supply workers. How does this work?

5. What does soul winning do for a church's influence?

6. What can an expanding church do for the community?

7. What is the church's number one business?

8. How has this lesson helped you?

23

CLOSING THE BACK DOOR OF THE CHURCH

"For it would be better for them not to have known the way of righteousness, than having known it, to turn away from the holy commandment delivered to them." II Peter 2:21

Another concern that the church faces today is the loss of its new members. Many churches experience a loss of their converts. After they come in the front door of the church, actually 30 to 90 percent of them go right out the back door. The tragedy of the problem is that the people have simply been given an innoculation against the gospel. They have tried conversion, and yet conversion was not real; in essence, they have been made immune to the gospel and their life state is worse than at the first.

Dawson Trotman, the founder of The Navigators, said:

> He soon found to be true something he learned from the men who brought him to the Saviour and from the book they studied — that leading a man to Christ is only a small part of the job. A man with heart prepared by the Spirit could make his decision for Christ in moments, but it was what went before and the months of patient work that followed that really counted.[1]

---

1. Dawson Trotman, *Making Your Witness Count,* (Colorado Springs, Colorado: Navpress, 1953), p. 1, (used by permission, SEND International, Farmington, MI).

With integrity, the church needs to deal with the new converts that come into its body. A suggestion that has been proven effective in many churches is the "buddy system" for all new converts or new families that come into the body. The very first Sunday, when the decision is made to become a Christian or part of the church, they are assigned another family who will stay with them through the first six to eight weeks of their membership. This "buddy family" will sit with them, will introduce them to their proper Sunday School classes, will introduce them to the prayer meetings, and Bible study groups of the church. It is their responsibility to see that the children get into the proper classes. During the first few weeks of their being in the church, they will be invited to dinner in the home of their shepherds. In general, the shepherd sees that the person does not feel left out when they come into the church. They are still made to feel important and not dropped immediately upon becoming a part of the fellowship.

The shepherd is assigned to people of similar age and interest, so that a young person is not assigned a buddy who is an old person, unless the old person relates very well to young people or vice versa. People should either volunteer or be asked to serve in the capacity of a buddy, but at the same time they must perform their work well once they have agreed to do so. A list of responsibilities to be performed on behalf of the members of the church should be typed up and supplied to each person who is going to act as a buddy.

A second means that can be used to help close the back door of the church is quality Bible preaching. It has been estimated that preaching topically through the Bible takes 1500 years. Unfortunately, the average person does not have that much time to learn about Jesus Christ and His plan for his life. Churches must do away with topical preaching and get back to preaching the Word of God. Preaching must be preaching, not just a Bible study or a lecture on the Bible. Expository preaching can be interesting. Preaching through the Bible books can bring new life to a church. The church ignorant of the Bible will become a thing of the past. People will begin to use their Bibles. It will become an open book.

An excellent textbook on the subject of expository preaching is *Expository Preaching Without Notes*,[2] by Charles W. Koller. This book

---

2. Charles W. Koller, *Expository Preaching Without Notes*, (Grand Rapids, Michigan: Baker Book House, 1962).

would be an asset to the average preacher. It would help him to close the back door of the church, since people will become interested in the continuity of what is being preached and will come Sunday after Sunday to learn about the content of a Bible book. This, supplemented with good Bible teaching in the Sunday School, will give the people a balanced diet so that they will grow in Christ, rather than fall by the wayside because of improper diet.

A third suggestion is to teach the Bible to the new convert. Every new person that comes into the church should be given a complete survey course of the Bible in the first year of their being a part of the body.[3] The lessons should begin with how the Bible is divided and is made up of the Old and New Testament scriptures with a brief explanation as to the significance of these facts. The Old Testament is divided into five sections, with five books of law, twelve books of history, five books of poetry, five books of major prophets, and twelve books of minor prophets.

The New Testament is divided into four books of biography, one book of history, twenty-one epistles, and the book of Revelation. Prophecy always stands last in the order of scripture.

The student should be given an introduction to the Bible. The Bible is not really one book, but sixty-six books, written by nearly forty different authors over a period of 1500 years in three different languages on three different continents. They should be introduced to why the Bible is the inspired word of God, why we believe it to be the word of God, with such evidence as its prophetic, scientific, historical, and factual accuracy. How it meets human needs should be shown.

Then the Bible books should be discussed briefly, one by one, giving an inside view of each Bible book's contents. For example, the book of Genesis means the book of beginnings. It deals with the beginning of nearly all things we know in the natural order of things; the beginning of the sun, moon, stars, animal and plant life, and humans themselves. It is made up of fifty chapters, with the first twelve chapters taking place before the time of Abraham and giving us a beginning of most things that have already been mentioned. The last thirty-eight chapters of the book of Genesis deal with the four great patriarchs, Abraham, Isaac,

---

3. Orrin Root, *Training for Service: A Survey of the Bible,* (Cincinnati, Ohio: Standard Publishing, 1964).

Jacob and Joseph. The new Christian can learn this quite easily and it will be a foundation for further reading.

The book of Exodus has forty chapters and is the story of the exiting of the children of Israel from Egypt. The first twelve chapters of the book deal with the children of Israel as they leave Egypt until they come to Mt. Sinai. It is "exit-us," the exit of the children of Israel from Egypt. In such manner, using key words and phrases, go on through the Bible. With a little research, each Bible book can be given a simple little outline that will be remembered by the people, to make the Bible a usable book.

As one progresses through the Bible, it is very important to show that the Bible is really a book about Jesus Christ. One can begin at Genesis 1:1 where the word, *Elohim* (the masculine plural noun actually meaning Gods), is used. This represents the Father, the Son and the Holy Spirit, working together in creation. Jesus is there working to create as John 1:1 tells us. Jesus is in Genesis 1:1.

Such stories as Abraham with his son Isaac show that God would one day offer His only Son near Mt. Moriah as a sacrifice for sin. He did not expect father Abraham to offer Isaac, but wanted the world to know how it would be for a man to offer his only son as a sacrifice for sin.

Many of the prophecies of the Old Testament need to be pointed out showing how they picture the coming of Jesus Christ one day. Using this means of study, the whole Bible should be reviewed, book by book, introducing them to it and helping them to understand how it all fits together into one whole. Also during this survey, historical, archaeological, and scientific truth can be shown. When the Bible has been completed, it is helpful to teach about Bible dispensations. See the chart on page 234 which shows the Bible dispensations and also gives a brief explanation as to how the chart ought to be taught.

Following a discussion of the Bible dispensations, there should be a discussion of the church revealed in the scriptures. Many people are not aware what the scriptures teach about the church and that there is a plan for this church. The plan is quite simple and easily followed and can bring great blessings to the life. The chart on page 142 is a suggested outline of the teaching on this subject. A discussion of eschatology, what happens to a person when he dies, can be very helpful in acquainting the person with the teaching of scripture. The chart on page 236 is suggested as a basis for this teaching.

232

At the conclusion of the class should be a discussion of what a person must do to become a Christian, remembering that the class is only a survey of the Bible to acquaint the person with the Bible's basic content. They can study it intelligently as they go to the other teaching classes of the church.

It has been the author's experience that with the preceding plan being implemented in the church, the church has been able to maintain about 80-90 percent of those who make the good confession. Those lost by moving away, of course, would not be included. About 10-20 percent of the people who become Christians will fall by the wayside. This is not desirable, but it is a reality of life that many people will make a decision and not be able to follow it through. If a church can maintain 90 percent of those who become Christians, it is ministering with integrity. That church, small or large, will be a blessing to the community which it serves.

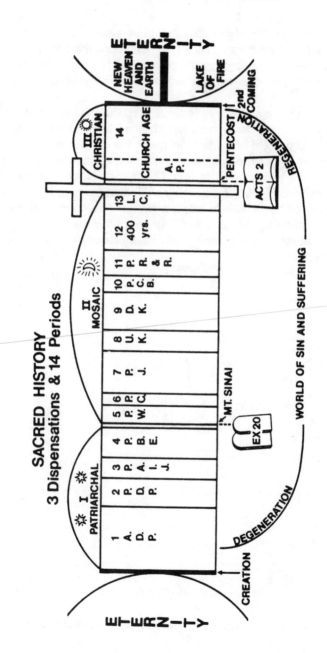

SACRED HISTORY
3 Dispensations & 14 Periods

Explanation Of The
Sacred History Chart

The three large arches across the top are the three great dispensations in God's program between creation and Christ's second coming.

The periods of sacred history within the dispensation are indicated by abbreviations. The Scriptures given below are the sections of scripture written during or pertaining to each period.

1. A.D.P. (Antediluvian period, or period before flood). Mankind went rapidly into sin (Gen. 1-8). Because of the wickedness of men, God destroyed the world by the flood. This period lasted over 1600 years.

2. P.D.P. (Postdiluvian period, or period after flood). Man went back into sin after the flood (Gen. 9-11).

3. P.A.I.J. (Period of Abraham, Isaac and Jacob). God called Abraham and his family. In them all nations were to be blessed (Gen. 12-50; Book of Job).

4. P.B.E. (Period of bondage). 400 years in Egypt (Exodus 1-12).

5. P.W. (Period of wandering). 40 years in the desert (Exodus 13-40; Lev.; Num.; and Deut.).

6. P.C. (Period of conquest). (Joshua).

7. P.J. (Period of judges). (Judges, Ruth and I Samuel 1-7).

8. U.K. (United kingdom). Reigns of Saul, David and Solomon (I Sam. 8-31; II Sam.; I Kings 1-11; I Chron. 10-20; II Chron. 1-9).

9. D.K. (Divided kingdom). Kingdoms of Judah and Israel (I Kings 12-22; II Kings: II Chron. 10-36). Prophetic books of Isaiah, Jeremiah, Lamentations, Hosea, Joel, Amos, Obadiah, Jonah, Micah, Nahum, Habakkuk and Zephaniah are from this period.

10. P.C.B. Period of Captivity in Babylon. 70 years in Babylon (Books of Daniel and Ezekiel; Psalm 137).

11. P.R.&R. (Period of Return and Restoration). (Ezra, Nehemiah, Esther, Haggai, Zechariah, Malachi).

12. 400 years between O.T. and N.T.

13. L.C. (Life of Christ). (Matthew, Mark, Luke, John).

14. Church age. (Acts, Epistles, Romans through Jude, and part of Revelation). During this age men can receive Christ, and be saved from the world. The first part of the church age (to about 100 A.D.) was the A.P., Apostolic period.

(This chart is from *Old Testament History*, College Press Publishing Co., 1986.)

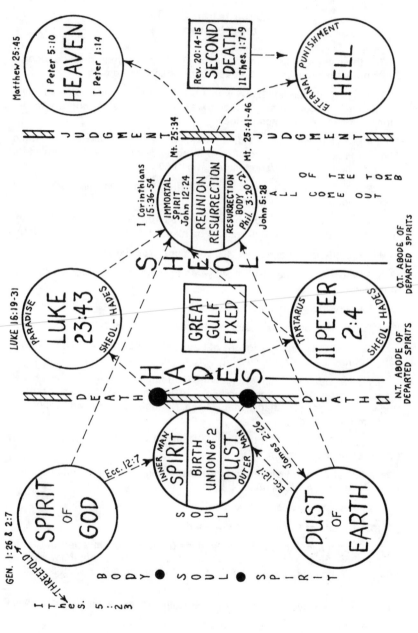

Chapter 23 Examination

1. What is meant by "closing the back door of the church?"

2. What percent of new converts are lost to Christ after conversion in many churches?

3. Which is easier, leading a person to Christ, or helping them to become mature in Christ?

4. What is the "buddy system" and how can it work in the church?

5. Why is expositional Bible preaching so important in closing the back door of the church?

6. Explain briefly, how a new convert can be taught the whole Bible in his first year as a Christian.

7. How many authors wrote the Bible? How many books are there in it? List the major subject divisions in the Bible.

8. What was the offering of Isaac illustrating? What does this illustrate about teaching a new Christian?

9. What is eschatology?

10. With proper teaching and orientation into the church, what percent can be kept faithful to Christ according to our text?

24

CONCLUSION

What will happen among our churches in the few remaining years of the twentieth century? Will we continue on in our unproductive methods or will we turn again to the Word of God to discover the principles that made the church so effective in its early years?

Will the church persist in floundering along in its divided state? Will churches continue apathetically on with little or no growth, anesthetized to the plan and desires of our Lord?

A new day must dawn on us! Never before in the whole history of the church has such opportunity been open to the church. Hardly a land on earth is closed to the gospel today. We have financial resources such as no other era of the church has had. Modern technology has given us many new tools. Inexpensive and rapid travel makes it possible to put personnel where they are needed most and quickly. Educational institutions are in place to train workers. Things are in position for the best days of the church.

The key to whether we will be able to take advantage of these opportunities is discipleship. The thread that runs throughout every part of this book is discipleship, the multiplication of workers for Christ. This is not easily done, it is time consuming, begins slowly, but will change the world. The principles endorsed in this book have been tried in the fires of experience; they work. If many churches will adopt them, then a new era will be begun in our fundamental churches.

The author realizes that these are only preliminary studies and his prayer is that some of the bright, new, young minds will take up the study and work. When the church member and student can be gotten out of the church and classroom into the harvest field, the church can again be and will be the dynamic force Christ wants it to be.

"Go therefore and make *disciples* of all the nations. . . ."[1]

1. Matthew 28:19.

Chapter 24 Examination

1. Where can we find the principles that made the church so effective in the first century? What was the number one principle?

2. Describe the opportunity before us in the words of our text.

3. What is the key doctrine that can turn around the church today, making it effective?

4. Discipleship will do what for our churches?

5. What must be done with our church members and students, if we are to see renewal of the church?

6. Write from memory, Matthew 28:18-20.

7. Think carefully about what has been left out of this book. Write a brief paragraph showing original or additional insights you might have on this subject.

8. What is the main good you have gotten out of this study?

9. How has your thinking been changed?

10. How has your life been changed?

Final Examination

1. What is God's purpose in the church?

2. What is the New Testament theology of church growth?

3. List twelve church growth principles.

4. Briefly, describe the perspective, programming and product of a Systems I, II and III type church.

5. Give a full definition of the New Testament word "disciple."

6. What one ingredient in the life of the great church discussed in chapter six was responsible for its quality growth?

7. How can II Corinthians 5:20 help you overcome timidity in personal evangelism?

8. Give four things as given in our text, that help motivate us to personal evangelism.

9. Show your weekly schedule and especially how you have set special times for personal evangelism in your life.

10. List four types of calls and the seven steps of a calling interview.

11. Give the scripture references for the Roman Road to Salvation.

12. What tools would you use to help teach a denominational person about the New Testament church?

13. What is the big issue in leading a Catholic to Christ?

14. What is the foundational error with the cults in general?

15. What do Mormons believe about the Bible?

16. Give ten ways a person can find prospects according to our text.

17. Give an illustration of using a unique way of opening a conversation about Christ.

18. What often hinders a preacher or church worker from being a soul winner?

19. _____True. _____False. The hospital is a very good place for in-depth personal evangelism and teaching.

20. What is the big issue to stick to in personal evangelism?

21. Give a brief plan for organizing "Bold Ones" in your church.

22. Explain briefly, how soul winning can work as a "cure all" for many church problems.

23. What is meant by "closing the back door of the church" and briefly, how can it be done?

24. What can discipleship do for our churches?

25. How has this class changed your life and thinking?

BIBLIOGRAPHY

Baker, Gordon Pratt. *A Year of Evangelism in the Local Church*. Nashville: Tidings Material for Christian Evangelism, 1960.

Benjamin, Paul. *The Growing Congregation*. Lincoln, Illinois: Lincoln Christian College Press, 1972.

Benjamin, Paul. *How In the World*. Lincoln, Illinois: Lincoln Christian College Press, 1973.

Bisagno, John. *How to Build An Evangelistic Church*. Nashville: Broadman Press, 1971.

Bright, Bill. *How to Fulfill the Great Commission*. San Bernardino, California: Campus Crusade, 1972.

Bright, Bill. *How to Introduce Others to Christ*. San Bernardino, California: Campus Crusade, 1972.

Broadhurst, C.N. *Personal Work or Bringing Men to Christ*. Cincinnati: Jennings and Graham, 1912.

Bryan, Dawson C. *They Went Forth Two by Two*. Nashville: Tidings, 1952.

Calkins, Raymond. *How Jesus Dealt With Men*. Nashville: Abingdon-Cokesbury Press, 1942.

Chalmers, Allan Knight. *As He Passed By*. New York: The Abingdon Press, 1939.

Coleman, Robert E. *The Master Plan of Evangelism*. Old Tappan, New Jersey: Fleming H. Revell, 1963.

Cooper, R.W. *Modern Evangelism*. New York: Fleming H. Revell, 1929.

Crane, Charles A. *Do You Know What the Mormon Church Teaches?* Grand Junction, Colorado: Intermountain Bible College Press, 1974.

Crane, Charles A. *The Bible and Mormon Scriptures Compared*. Joplin, Missouri: College Press, 1983 Revised Edition.

Davis, Ozora. *Meeting the Master*. New York: Association Press, 1917.

Dean, Horace. *Visitation Evangelism Made Practical*. Grand Rapids, Michigan: Zondervan, 1955.

Downey, Murray W. *The Art of Soul Winning*. Grand Rapids, Michigan: Baker Book House, 1957.

Edwards, Gene. *How to Have A Soul Winning Church*. Tyler, Texas: Soul Winning Publications, 1963.

Ellis, Joe. *The Personal Evangelist*. Cincinnati, Ohio: Standard Publishing, 1964.

"Evangelism — the Mission of the Church to Those Outside Her Life," by Theodore O. Wedel. Paraphrased by Richard Wheatcroft, *Letters to Laymen*. Cited by Howard Clinebell, Jr., *Basic Types of Pastoral Counselling*. Nashville: Abingdon Press, 1966.

Evans, William. *Personal Soul Winning*. Chicago: Moody Press, 1964.

Gatewood, Otis. *You Can Do Personal Work*. Otis Gatewood, publisher, 1956.

Hailey, Homer. *Let's Go Fishing For Men*. Abilene, Texas: Quality

Printing Co., 1951.

Henrichsen, Walter A. *Disciples Are Made — Not Born.* Wheaton, Illinois: SP Publications, 1974.

Hodges, Melvin L. *The Indigenous Church.* Springfield, Missouri: Gospel Publishing House, 1953.

Hyles, Jack. *Let's Baptize More Converts.* Murfreesboro, Tennessee: Sword of the Lord, 1967.

Hyles, Jack. *Let's Build An Evangelistic Church.* Murfreesboro, Tennessee: Sword of the Lord, 1962.

Hyles, Jack. *Let's Go Soul Winning.* Murfreesboro, Tennessee: Sword of the Lord, 1962.

Jauncey, James. *Psychology for Successful Evangelism.* Chicago: Moody Press, 1972.

Kennedy, D.Y. *Evangelism Explosion.* Wheaton, Illinois: Tyndale Publishing House, 1970.

Koller, Charles W. *Expository Preaching Without Notes.* Grand Rapids, Michigan: Baker Book House. 1962.

Kubler-Ross, Elisabeth. *On Death and Dying.* New York: The Macmillan Company, 1969.

LaSor, William Sanford. *The Dead Sea Scrolls.* Chicago: Moody Press, 1962.

Lee, Robert G. *How to Lead A Soul to Christ.* Grand Rapids, Michigan: Zondervan, 1955.

Little, Paul. *How to Give Away Your Faith.* Chicago: Intervarsity Press, 1966.

Lovett, C.S. *Soul Winning is Easy.* Grand Rapids, Michigan: Zondervan, 1976.

Malone, Tom. *Essentials of Evangelism.* Grand Rapids: Kregel Publications, 1958.

Mayfield, William A. *Restoring New Testament Evangelism.* Melvourne, Florida: New Life Books, 1974.

McBirney, William S. *The Search for the Twelve Apostles.* Wheaton, Illinois: Tyndale Publishing House, 1969.

McFatridge, F. V. *The Personal Evangelism of Jesus.* Grand Rapids, Michigan: Zondervan, 1939.

McGavran, Donald and Arn, Win. *How to Grow A Church.* Glendale, California: Regal Books, 1973.

Miller, H. S. *General Biblical Introduction.* Houghton: New York: The Word Bearer Press, 1959.

Moorhous, Carl W. *Growing New Churches.* Gary, Indiana: Carl Moorhous, publisher, 1975.

Morgan, G. Campbell. *The Great Physician.* New York: Fleming H. Revell Company, 1937.

Nock, A. D. *Conversion.* London-Oxford-New York: Oxford University Press, 1972.

Parmenter, Bruce. *The Healing of Our Grief.* Lincoln, Illinois: Bruce Parmenter, publisher, 1974.

Religious Truths Defined, p. 175 and 337. Cited by Jerald Tanner and Sandra Tanner. *Mormonism — Shadow or Reality?* p. 64. Salt Lake City, Utah: Modern Microfilm Company, 1964.

Rice, John R. *742 Heart-Warming Poems.* Murfreesboro, Tennessee: Sword of the Lord Publishers, 1972.

Rinker, Rosalind. *You Can Witness With Confidence.* Grand Rapids, Michigan: Zondervan, 1962.

Roberts, B.H., ed. *History of the Church of Jesus Christ of Latter-Day Saints.* 7 Vols. 2nd ed. rev. Salt Lake City, Utah: Deseret News Press, 1963.

Root, Orrin. *Training for Service: A Survey of the Bible.* Cincinnati, Ohio: Standard Publishing Co., 1964.

Rosen, Martin Meyer. *How to Witness Simply and Effectively to the Jews.* 236 West 72 Street, New York: American Board of Missions to The Jews, Inc.

Sanny, Lorne. *Outlines in Personal Evangelism.* Lincoln, Nebraska: Back to Bible Broadcast, 1972.

Scarborough, L.R. *How Jesus Won Man.* New York: George H. Doran Co., 1926.

Sharp, C.J. *New Testament Evangelism.* Cincinnati: Standard Publishing Company, 1941.

Sisemore, John T. *The Ministry of Visitation.* Nashville: Broadman Press, 1954.

Sligh, John Calhoun. *Christ's Way of Winning Souls.* Nashville: Publishing House of the Methodist Episcopal Church, South, 1909.

Smith, Alfred B., ed. *Inspiring Hymns.* Wheaton, Illinois: Singspiration, 1951.

Smith, John C. *The Magnetism of Christ.* London: Hodder and Stoughton, 1904.

Steward, Robert Ivan. *From House to House.* Rosemead, California: Old Path Book Club, 1956.

Stokes, Mack. *The Evangelism of Jesus.* Nashville: Methodist Evangelistic Materials, 1960.

Stone, John Timothy. *Recruiting For Christ.* London: Fleming H. Revell, Co., 1910.

The Atonement Between God and Man. Watchtower

Todd, Cecil; Thomas, Reggie; Martin, Russ; Laue, William. *The Technique of Soul Winning.* Joplin, Missouri: Revival Fires, 1968.

Torrey, R.A. *Vest Pocket Companion for Christian Workers.* Grand Rapids, Michigan: Zondervan, 1976.

Towns, Elmer. *The Successful Sunday School and Teachers Guidebook.* Carol Stream, Illinois: Creation House, 1976.

Trotman, Dawson. *Making Your Witness Count.* Colorado Springs, Colorado: Navpress, 1953.

Trueblood, Elton. *The Company of the Committed.* New York: Harper and Row, 1961.

Trumbull, Charles G. *Taking Men Alive.* New York: Fleming H. Revell, 1938.

Vine, W.E. *Expository Dictionary of New Testament Words.* Westwood, New Jersey: Fleming H. Revell Company, 1958.

Wareing, Earnest Clyde. *The Evangelism of Jesus.* New York: The Abingdon Press, 1918.

Watson, L. Arnold. *The Personal Worker's Manual.* Abilene, Texas: Fidelity Book and Supply, 1965.

Westbery, Granger. *Good Grief.* Philadelphia: Fortress Press, 1962.

White, Willie. *Willie White's Program of Comprehensive Evangelism.* Cincinnati, Ohio: Standard Publishing Co., 1960.

Whitesell, Faris D. *Basic New Testament Evangelism.* Grand Rapids, Michigan: Zondervan, 1949.

Wilson, Walter L. *Let's Go Fishing.* Findley, Ohio: Dunham Publishing Co., 1938.

Yadan, Yigael. *Masada.* 3032 Grays Inn Road, London: Sphere Books Limited.

Yamamori, Tetsunao and Lawson, E. LeRoy. *Introducing Church Growth.* Cincinnati, Ohio: Standard Publishing Co., 1975.